"*The Gift of Anger* is a concise and easily followed guide to understanding and managing anger. By weaving together simple and graspable case examples and insightful broad principles, Marcia Cannon shows us a way to enhance our emotional competence in an important domain."

—Frederic Luskin, Ph.D., director of Stanford Forgiveness Project and author of *Forgive for Good*

"Cannon's book is an invaluable tool for thoroughly and soulfully mining the experience of anger for all of its gifts of insight, depth, and growth."

—Kathy Carlson, Ph.D., MFT, psychotherapist, writer, and documentary filmmaker

"No anger is needed to benefit from reading this exceptional book. This is a manual written by a gifted therapist who looks at the positive effects anger can have on one's life."

—Linda L. Haase, ABT, RM is an Asian Bodywork therapist and Reiki master in Johns Creek, GA

"*The Gift of Anger* takes us by the hand and leads us step by step through one brilliant insight after another. In all my years as a psychotherapist, I have never encountered this level of clarity and wisdom about anger. This powerful book is destined to become a classic."

—Belinda Gore, Ph.D., leadership consultant and coach, director of The Enneagram Institute of Central Ohio, and president of The Cuyamungue Institute, Santa Fe, NM

"The concepts in Cannon's *The Gift of Anger* are sound and research-tested, but the true gift is in her straightforward and simple-to-follow presentation. The book is grounded in psychological and spiritual truths that transcend religious boundaries, and therefore it is suitable for any faith community or secular group."

—David Hett, Ph.D., Minister of Religious Life and Learning at First Community Church

"This book is brilliant, easy to read, and deeply intelligent. I was compelled from start to finish by its warmth, wisdom, and truth. No matter where you are in life, the teachings in this book will speak directly to you."

—Barbara Reiner, Spiritual Awareness Counseling

"*The Gift of Anger* is both intelligent and accessible, two of the most highly valued qualities I look for in books I read and recommend to my clients and students. Cannon presents concrete steps for moving from anger to empowerment. Even though this book is written clearly and simply, it also deeply explores the function of anger in the human mind. A must-read for understanding the inner journey."

—Marla Estes, founder of The School of the Examined Life

"*The Gift of Anger* offers a seven-step process based on perennial wisdoms that motivates us to work with anger honestly and directly, without doing harm to ourselves and others. This book is a practical guide that supports healing, justice, and ignites positive change for all concerned."

—Angeles Arrien, Ph.D., cultural anthropologist and award-winning author

"What a powerful approach to befriending anger and using it to enhance well-being! Reading and working with this material provides an opportunity for dealing with one's anger in a totally new light. Through a wonderful combination of clear explanations, case study examples, and personal exercises, Cannon provides the reader with a step-by-step guide to a very rich practice for expanding self-awareness and compassion for self and others. I look forward to reaping the benefits of this practice by incorporating it into my life and sharing the results, as well as this book, with others."

—Lynda Roberts, International Enneagram Association board member, director of the Enneagram Institute of Georgia, and leadership and management consultant

"All afflictive emotional states can be transformed, through care and attention, into sources of wisdom and compassion for ourselves and others. In *The Gift of Anger*, Cannon provides an insightful, thorough, and effective guide for transforming anger and developing clear, skillful, and generous relationships. Anyone wishing to understand this process would do well to read, reflect on, use, and enjoy this book."

—Rev. Daijaku Judith Kinst, Ph.D., Soto Zen Buddhist priest and teacher and assistant professor at the Institute of Buddhist Studies at the Graduate Theological Union in Berkeley, CA

"One of the great breakthroughs that the human potential movement has brought us is its amoral framework for negative emotions like anger, fear, and greed. To regard these as engineering issues rather than moral judgments on ourselves or others puts us in charge of our lives in a refreshing way that holds a great deal of potential for health and happiness. *The Gift of Anger* is a welcome contribution to this field. It lays out systematically how we can take control of our mental state and use the raw energy of anger (for such it is) in constructive ways. Considering that we are living in 'the Age of Anger' according to some wisdom traditions, this simple toolset could make quite a difference!"

—Michael Nagler, Ph.D., author of *In Search of a Nonviolent Future*

"Finally, a book that addresses a truly healthy and wise way to relate to anger. Cannon clearly and insightfully details a process for not only understanding and managing anger, but also using anger as a guide for personal growth and healing."

—Joyce Harris, MA, MFTI

"*The Gift of Anger* is a perfect resource for anyone who has wondered how to work with their anger. It shows us that anger can be a portal to a deeper and more real understanding of ourselves. Anger can truly be transformational when understood in the way that Cannon proposes. I recommend this book as a practical tool and an inspirational guide to anyone who is seeking truth."

—Kate Betteley, clinical psychologist

"I've been moved by the inner reach of Cannon's book. It provides a refreshing and wise, yet accessible approach to unraveling and under-standing the emotion of anger. As a talented teacher and therapist, Cannon takes the reader on a journey that is empowering, immensely satisfying, and healing for the soul. Use her practical guidance and insightful examples to discover how anger can be an important vehicle for authentic well-being."

—Roxanne Howe-Murphy, Ed.D., author of *Deep Coaching*

"Cannon has written a very useful workbook for self-reflection that will help readers sort out angry feelings and reactions that can impact their self-esteem and personal relationships."

—Suzy Spradlin, Ph.D., Jungian analyst

"In *The Gift of Anger*, Cannon has given us a very specific method for transforming angry feelings into expanded self-awareness. The step-by-step structured exercises guide the reader to deeply explore this complex emotion with the openness and self-compassion that are necessary for change."

> —Bonnie Payne, Ph.D., psychologist and Jungian analyst in private practice in Los Gatos, CA

"This book takes that most difficult of emotions, anger, shows us how to deal with it, and turns it into a valuable tool for insight. It made my anger a lot less scary and a lot more manageable. My reaction now is going to be 'Oh, here comes anger, I wonder why?' instead of my more habitual reaction of ignoring anger when it shows up. I recommend this book to anyone who is on the path of self-understanding, even those who don't think that anger is a problem. They will find that anger can be a shortcut to self-discovery."

> —Tom Flautt, Ph.D., past president of International Enneagram Association

"Many of us have learned how to manage our anger, but learning how to transform our anger into a gift is a whole new concept. This book guides the participant into realizing how to do just that. Each chapter is rich with discussion, insight, and practices that clearly demonstrate how we can learn to harness anger for the gift of personal growth and development. I have used this model or aspects of it many times; it has never failed me. I heartily recommend *The Gift of Anger* to anyone who chooses to become a more peaceful, whole human being."

> —Mary Powers, former client and orientation and mobility specialist for people with vision loss and blindness

"*The Gift of Anger* provides a reassuring and practical road map for bringing us greater self-awareness and peaceful living. Using the seven-step process clearly outlined in the book, I have moved through my own experiences of anger with more clarity and kindness towards myself and others. Cannon is a wise, compassionate guide and teacher and truly shines a light on the path of this journey!"

> —Gerianne Hummel, former client, Reiki master teacher, and owner of Essential Elements Aromatherapy

the gift of anger

7 Steps to Uncover the Meaning
of Anger and Gain Awareness,
True Strength, and Peace

Marcia Cannon, Ph.D.

New Harbinger Publications, Inc.

Publisher's Note

This publication is designed to provide accurate and authoritative information in regard to the subject matter covered. It is sold with the understanding that the publisher is not engaged in rendering psychological, financial, legal, or other professional services. If expert assistance or counseling is needed, the services of a competent professional should be sought.

Distributed in Canada by Raincoast Books

Copyright © 2011 by Marcia Cannon
New Harbinger Publications, Inc.
5674 Shattuck Avenue
Oakland, CA 94609
www.newharbinger.com

FSC
Mixed Sources
Product group from well-managed
forests and other controlled sources

Cert no. SW-COC-002283
www.fsc.org
© 1996 Forest Stewardship Council

Acquired by Tesilya Hanauer; Cover design by Amy Shoup; Edited by Carole Honeychurch

Library of Congress Cataloging-in-Publication Data

Cannon, Marcia G.
  The gift of anger : seven steps to uncover the meaning of anger and gain awareness, true strength, and peace / Marcia G. Cannon.
     p. cm.
  Includes bibliographical references.
  ISBN 978-1-57224-966-0 (pbk.) -- ISBN 978-1-57224-967-7 (pdf ebook) 1. Anger. 2. Self-actualization (Psychology) I. Title.
  BF575.A5C36 2011
  152.4'7--dc22

                                         2010050889

Contents

Acknowledgments

So many people helped make this book a reality. I want to thank my clients and workshop participants, who enriched this book with their stories and taught me as much as I taught them. I also want to thank my family, friends, and colleagues, who offered support throughout the writing process and spurred me on by asking when they could have a copy of this book.

Thanks to all of you at New Harbinger Publications, especially Tesilya Hanauer and Jesse Beebe, for your trust, your help, and your dedicated work.

Special thanks go to my son Gary Kurtzman, who critiqued each chapter and helped me rearrange my thoughts into an order that flowed well. I don't know where you found the time, Gary, but this book has clearly benefited from your suggestions, and I'm very grateful!

I especially want to thank my husband, Kelly, who talked through all the concepts with me, edited the chapters, and most importantly, kept me relatively sane throughout this new and challenging process. Thank you for your unfailing humor, Kel, and for your ongoing patience, understanding, and support. Most of all, thank you for the love and joy you bring me and for being the amazingly wonderful person you are.

Most of all, I want to thank you, the reader. It is for you that this book is written. May the ideas and process contained here lead you to appreciate all of your emotions as you enjoy a deeper sense of peace.

Introduction:
A New Understanding

"It's nothing I can't handle," Amy assured me as she described how frequently she felt irritated at work. "I'm sure it's just normal. Right?"

*

"All my life my sister's been the needy one who's gotten all the attention," Linda complained resentfully. "Why can't my mother ever ask me if I need anything? And why can't my sister just grow up?"

*

"I've had it with these damn meetings!" Fred fumed. "How do they expect me to get any work done when I'm sitting in conference rooms all day?"

*

Anger. As these brief quotes illustrate, it comes in a range of strengths, from mild irritation, to frustration, all the way to fury and rage. In one form or another, one thing is for sure—we all get angry. When we do, we are often taught by conventional wisdom that what we feel is bad or dangerous, and that we should manage our anger and hopefully get rid of it. But what if conventional wisdom is wrong? What if anger, like all of our other emotions, can be positive, useful, and a guide to our own increased well-being? What if, rather than being a problem, your anger can be a gift?

The Need for This Book

I wrote *The Gift of Anger* as an antidote to the negativity and misunderstanding that so often surround this emotion. I wrote it to show you a positive, more useful definition of anger and a process for working with it that is not only satisfying but healing and empowering as well. Whether you are mildly frustrated, outright furious, or anything in between, you will learn how to use your anger creatively and effectively—not to hurt your neighbor but to heal and help yourself. Using the information and techniques in this book can help you become stronger and more positively connected, both with yourself and to the world around you.

It is time to move beyond the shame or fear associated with this emotion. It is time to embrace your anger constructively and learn how to use it to achieve the very goals that most people wish for—decreasing pain and increasing your sense of personal effectiveness and empowerment. Stated differently and more personally, it's time to feel really good about yourself. I'm not talking about the superficial and momentary boost that an angry outburst can grant; instead, by using your anger to help you uncover and integrate a more accurate and positive definition of yourself and of the world around you, you will gain a deep and long-lasting sense of achievement and well-being.

This is not a book about communicating with others to resolve your anger. While that is a worthwhile subject, there already are a number of good books on interpersonal communication and anger management. *The Gift of Anger* is different. It invites you to communicate with *yourself* and shows you how to do so in a way that makes use of the positive potential of your anger while dissolving its negative impulse. The process you'll learn will heighten your awareness of yourself as it helps you to uncover the true purpose of your anger and learn how to use all of your emotions in ways that further your understanding, your self-confidence, and your sense of inner and interpersonal harmony.

This is a book for all of us who know we get angry and wish we could use our anger positively rather than just containing it, acting it out, stuffing it back inside, or somehow getting through it. This book is also for each of us who carry around old or new resentments, wishing we could be rid of them but not knowing how. It is, as well, a book for those of us who believe we almost never become angry but perhaps feel hurt, tired, overwhelmed, or depressed by some of our encounters with other people. In fact, this is a book for everyone who wants to gain a better understanding of anger, an understanding that begins by exploring the two stages of anger.

A Brief Introduction to the Two Stages of Anger

What you have learned to call "anger" is actually only its first stage, the *protective stage*. Here, your anger gives you a power boost to make you feel bigger and stronger so that you can face a person who seems more powerful than you or a situation that seems too difficult to manage. But this is only stage one. Anger has a second stage, one that is at least as potent as the first, though much less well known. The second stage, the *awareness and growth stage*, is quieter and more thoughtful than stage one. This is a time when your anger can become an unerring guide to healing your emotional pain. It will enhance both your sense of well-being and your capacity to respond more calmly and successfully to the inevitable changes and difficulties that are part of everyone's life.

While the first, protective stage of anger is automatic, showing up whether you want it to or not, the second stage is optional. To reap the benefits of stage two, you have to consciously choose it. This book will show you how.

Chapter 1 of *The Gift of Anger* examines the first (protective) stage of your anger, while chapters 2 and 3 focus on the second (awareness and growth) stage. You will explore the often-overlooked attributes that make your anger so valuable when you choose to use it in stage two. You will delve deeply into how anger is created and learn how the very ingredients that cause anger can be used to help you heal from your angering experiences and empower you to move beyond them.

The next seven chapters, the heart of the book, are devoted to teaching a seven-step process that makes full use of the potential of anger for increasing awareness and assisting personal growth. Using this process, you can reduce the emotional pain associated with your anger, gain self-awareness from your anger, and move more deeply into a state of personal and interpersonal peace. In each of these chapters, I explain one of the seven steps of this process, offer examples of its use, and then provide exercises that allow you to personalize the information by exploring yourself and your anger as deeply and fully as you wish. The final chapter shows you how to use this process when you are angry with yourself.

As you do the chapter exercises, it will be helpful to write them down. Consider doing so in a journal that you dedicate to recording the discoveries you make about yourself and about your anger as you complete each exercise. Doing so, you will have all the information you gain about your anger in one place so that you can easily refer back to it as needed and track your progress as well.

The seven-step process you'll be learning establishes a blueprint for working with your anger from the moment that you first become aware of feeling something upsetting to the time when you feel more deeply and consciously at peace. You will explore specific steps to take and a specific order for taking them, and you can read about others who have offered their stories so that you can "see" these steps in action.

It's important to remember that the process is not focused on condoning bad behavior. In fact, the opposite is true. I'm sure that, like most people, you're aware of how difficult it can be to think clearly and speak effectively while under the influence of your own anger. The more you use the process in this book to understand your anger and heal its underlying causes, the more you will be calmer, stronger, and able to effectively address whatever person or situation you're facing.

With the techniques you learn here, you can use your anger positively, with less risk to your relationships. You can learn how to experience anger as a step on a path toward growth, a step that can lead you to a deepened sense of inner and interpersonal peace and understanding and a heightened sense of well-being.

If You Need Help

While this process can help in any angry situation, it is not meant as a substitute for professional counseling. If you have a serious issue, such as working through anger that causes or results from violence, I encourage you to see a professional counselor. When life experiences are traumatic, the kindest and often most effective way to work through them is with the supportive help of a well-trained professional. The same is true if you find that any of the exercises in this book bring up difficult emotions or memories. If that happens, a trained counselor can help you to use the experience as a deeper opportunity for healing.

Why I Wrote This Book

I did not personally invent any of the techniques in the seven-step process; they have been around longer than I have. What I did was to bring them together and integrate them in a specific way as I discovered what worked best, first for myself and then for clients.

I first learned some of the basic concepts many years ago when I was looking for ways to work with my own anger. Later, as a psychotherapist working with individual clients and with couples, I found that no matter what their reasons for coming to therapy, most of my clients needed help working through anger. I used the techniques I had learned and refined the process as I saw what was most helpful to clients. Over the years, in clinical settings and in private practice, I've used the process to help people transform their angry feelings into the self-confidence that awareness and personal growth brings.

When I began working on my Ph.D. in 1999 and needed to choose a dissertation topic, the gift-of-anger process seemed a natural choice. I did a controlled study using a small population and tested participants over time using the process I'm offering here. My goal was to measure both the immediate and long-term effects on participants' feelings and behavior.

The results of the study were exciting. People who took the training expressed relief and gratitude. They had finally found a positive way to work with their anger, a way that left them feeling strengthened, centered, and more at peace.

The people who learned the seven-step process made significant, positive changes in their attitude and behavior toward themselves and those with whom they had been angry, and they maintained those positive changes over time. Most exciting was the fact that study participants reported feeling both increased inner strength and a greater ability to handle the nasty surprises that life often delivers. Many said that they would never look at anger in the same way again.

The people I describe in this book are based on workshop attendees, study participants, and clients. I have changed their names and other information to protect their privacy, and I have used examples that I've found to be representative of many people's issues. I hope you will see yourself in some of these examples. When you do, please take heart in the fact that these people, using their anger and hurt as a starting point, turned their lives around. You, too, can use your anger as a starting point and let this process lead you to an increased sense of peace, strength, and compassion, both for yourself and for those around you. Anger can be a healing tool, a powerful initiator of positive change. That is its gift. It's time for each of us to understand our own anger that way and to use it wisely.

Our greatest ability to influence others is through example. When you use your anger as the positive force it was meant to be, then your increased self-awareness, inner healing, and heightened sense of confidence and peace will affect both you and those around you in ways that may surprise and delight you. That is the power of anger properly used. It can be your power. Just open your gift, and you'll see.

CHAPTER 1

Stage One: Anger As a Protective Reaction

Every living being needs some form of protection in order to survive. People are no different from animals in this respect. When the world seems hostile, anger is one of the defenses we humans use to protect ourselves. Like the spikes on a cactus or the thorns on a rose, anger is designed to keep us safe.

Anger is a built-in, natural emotion that everyone feels. Each of us, from youngest to oldest, is born with the ability to get mad, and it's not a shy emotion that waits to be asked to emerge. Like it or not, your anger comes up automatically when you need help to deal with a perceived threat or in seemingly tough situations that you don't feel powerful enough to handle calmly and easily.

The Power-Boost Effect

Anger pumps you up. It offers protection by increasing your power, giving you (at least temporarily) the extra strength you need to feel bigger, stronger, and more formidable. With the added strength of anger, you can gain safety by distancing yourself from the people around you, your anger acting as an imposing armor between you and the rest of the world.

You can feel this armor in a variety of strengths, depending on the level of your anger. You might think of anger as an "umbrella" term, because it covers a lot of seemingly different emotions. Annoyance, irritation, bitterness, exasperation, frustration, resentment, aggravation, indignation, fury, and rage are just some of the labels given to various intensities of anger, each one offering a different level of protection.

Anger also offers you protection by removing some of your inhibitions against using verbal or physical force so that you can take a firm stand when you feel it's necessary. With its added strength and lessening of inhibitions against using that strength, anger can enable and even compel you to speak a difficult truth you've been unable to express—to say no and mean it, even when you have previously been too scared to do so. While it can be misused, anger can give you courage, determination, and the willingness to set limits and take action. Consider the following examples.

⑾ Carolyn

Carolyn was tired but happy—so happy! She had been caring for her mom for months and now, *finally*, she was getting a vacation. Although she had a brother, Carolyn was the one who lived closest to their mother, and Carolyn was single. Unlike her brother, she could make no excuses about the long trip and its high cost, nor, since she was single, could she plead other family needs pulling her away. But finally her brother, Jerry, was taking time off from work and from his growing family to come and stay with their mother while Carolyn spent a week with a friend. *A week* she thought to herself, *a whole week. I can hardly wait!*

She was in the middle of imagining her long-awaited vacation when the phone rang. It was Jerry. Something about an unexpected project at work. He was in the middle of explaining when Carolyn broke in with her own words. "No!" she yelled into the phone. "You promised, and now you do it. Do you hear me? You just do it!" Carolyn's words were out before she could even think about them, before she even realized they were there. Shaking with unexpected fury, she took a deep breath and silently told herself to calm down.

Carolyn's unexpected anger gave her the power to command her brother to make the trip to take care of their mother, no matter what obstacles were in his way. It made her act strong and tough, considerably tougher than she normally felt. In the end, her anger was not enough to get her brother to keep his promise, but it did show them both that Carolyn needed help with their mother. As a result, after a number of discussions that ranged from heated and tearful to heartfelt, new caretaking arrangements were made that gave Carolyn set vacations that she could count on.

⎍⎍⎍ Steve

Steve sat in my office feeling remorseful. "I don't know what came over me," he said. "The driver stopped short and I almost hit him, and then he made a quick turn and took off. The next thing I knew I was enraged. I chased the guy to the stoplight and got out of my car to face him. I only came to my senses when I saw that the driver was a woman. I have no idea what I would have done if she'd been a man. I'm just glad we're both okay."

Talking further about what happened and about his life in general, Steve admitted that times were pretty tough. A building contractor newly out on his own, he'd been hit hard by an economic downturn. "I'm taking jobs helping other contractors," he said dejectedly, "but finding work is pretty tough. I'm worried about my business and about my bills. I'm worried about my future."

Scared about what might happen and about what he should—or could—do about it, Steve felt he was losing control over his life. He described it as feeling "at the mercy of whatever might come next." What came next was a woman driver who stopped quickly and then made a fast turn in her car. That was enough to galvanize and focus (or, in this case, mis-focus) his anger at his life's uncertainty.

Different Kinds of Protection

Through the power boost of anger, you can protect your self-image by fantasizing about reacting powerfully or take immediate action that you might not have thought you had the strength to take. Thus, Carolyn's anger gave her the power to stand up to her brother, something she had previously felt too weak to do. More than just provide the power, her anger demanded that she stand up to him and even took over and did the job for her. Then, her anger propelled her to discuss her need for caretaking help with her brother, a discussion she'd been nervous about having. Steve's anger gave him a momentary (though dangerously inappropriate) outlet for his fear and frustration at not knowing what his future would look like or what he could do about it. In my own case, as you will read below, my anger kept me safe.

⑪ Marcia

Years ago, I was working alone in an office when a man who was a stranger to me came in. He was tall and large and began speaking loudly and incoherently when he saw me. As he walked quickly toward me, I became afraid. He advanced, and I backed up until I realized that if I backed up any farther I would be trapped in a back office with this frightening stranger.

At that point, my fear turned to anger and the protective power boost from my emotion changed the situation completely. Speaking in a forceful, authoritative voice, I told the man it was time for him to leave. As I spoke, I walked purposefully toward him. "You have to leave now!" I said loudly and firmly, continuing to walk toward him. The balance of power shifted in that instant. As I advanced, he backed up. A few seconds later he was out the door, which I immediately locked.

My anger had been automatic. Had I thought about what I was doing, I don't think I would have had the courage to act. Actually, I don't even think I would have trusted that that behavior would work. When the power boost of anger takes charge, we often find ourselves acting without thinking. While in Steve's case, his anger resulted in dangerous behavior, in my case it may have saved me from harm.

Exploring Your Own Power Boost

Like the people in these examples, and like everyone else as well, you've undoubtedly gotten angry with others and had others become angry with you. If you are like many people, however, you may have done little objective exploration of your own anger, your own protective power boost. With the exercise that follows, you can begin this process, a journey of self-exploration that will continue throughout this book. The following exercise, and the exercises that come later, will enable you to explore your anger in depth and from different angles so you can understand it more thoroughly and use it safely and successfully to further your own well-being and growth.

As you read the exercise, consider approaching it and all of the other personal exercises in this book with what Buddhist philosophy calls *beginner's mind*. Starting with the idea that a mind already filled with information and answers has no room left to deeply explore a subject, consider gently moving aside whatever you already know about anger. Doing so, you can come to these exercises with a fresh mind, a beginner's mind, and see where the exercises take you. Then, as you complete this exercise and the ones that follow, write down what you have discovered about anger and about your own expression of anger in your anger journal, creating a central place to keep your observations and record your growing awareness.

This first exercise will help you personalize the idea of your anger as a protective power boost. Using the following questions, you can explore your own anger to see what caused it, how you used it, and how doing so affected you.

11

EXERCISE: An Experience of Anger

Think of a time when you became angry. Pick an experience that resulted in a fairly low level of anger, such as frustration or annoyance, rather than one resulting in more intense anger, such as fury or rage. Doing so, you can more objectively focus your attention on the questions below. When you have your experience clearly in mind, give yourself the time to thoughtfully answer the following:

1. Describe the situation briefly and review what it was about this experience that angered you.

2. Did the power boost of your anger protect you by propelling you to take a stand? Set limits? Take action? Something else?

3. What effect did your anger have on your level of courage? Your determination? Your estimation of yourself and of the other person/people?

4. Did becoming angry bring you the results you hoped for? If not, what did result? Is this result familiar?

Having answered the questions above, you have hopefully gained a more personal understanding of how the protective power boost of your anger works. Next, you can add to your understanding by exploring what triggers your anger. Frequently, three key factors work together to act as a trigger.

The Three Keys

The first of three key factors that usually work together to trigger anger is your *experience of a situation or behavior that you judge as unfair, hurtful, or in some other way "wrong."* This negative experience almost always involves someone or something not meeting expectations that are important to you, expectations that you value.

The second key factor in becoming angry is that you *feel unable to calmly and easily right the wrong.* Perhaps you believe that you lack the skill or the ability to do so, or perhaps the person or situation you're facing seems bigger and more powerful than you. If that is the case, you may be too frightened to confront the person calmly or discuss the problem with a cool head. You may also feel shocked by what has happened, and therefore temporarily overpowered or overwhelmed by the experience. In addition, you may be dealing with other recent experiences that have already strained your ability to respond calmly. Like Steve, who chased another driver in an earlier example, your current experience may be one problem too many. Whatever the reason, you are left feeling unable to resolve the problem calmly.

The third key factor that initiates anger is that *the experience is troubling enough that you cannot simply tolerate it or let it go.* It feels too big, too upsetting, and you feel caught in its grip.

Taken together, these three factors comprise a powerful combination of circumstances. First, you are faced with an experience that seems wrong or unfair. Second, you don't feel able to calmly correct it. And yet, in order for you to feel okay, the situation must be successfully resolved because leaving it as it is does not feel like an acceptable option (the third factor).

There is a moral sense to this trio of judgments, a belief that you or someone you care about deserved better. Most likely, you also have a sense of personal diminishment as a result of not being able to simply fix the problem. The situation has overpowered you, at least for that moment, and you feel weaker, smaller, and less in control as a result.

In this kind of predicament, you're left with a conflict. You feel a strong desire to right a situation that seems wrong, yet you also believe that, at least for now, you are unable to do so. When this set of circumstances occurs, your normal, built-in, human response is anger.

⑾ Jim

As an example, consider Jim. At age twenty-three, he is eager, energetic, and determined. Jim has worked diligently in his job for almost two years. He has carefully and thoroughly done everything asked of him, even though doing so involved countless hours of overtime. He has dedicated himself to his place of work and to his job there. Now he has learned that there is a possibility of promotion. Jim's colleague, who is one level up in the organization, is leaving, and the company needs a replacement. From the job description, it's clear to Jim that he more than meets the qualifications. Confidently, he waits for the call to his boss's office, expecting that at any moment it will come and he will be offered his new job.

You have probably figured out the rest of this story. Jim was furious at not getting the job he was sure he would get and certain that he deserved. "Those bastards," he stormed. "What were they thinking? I'm twice as good as Tom is. How could they give him my promotion? I worked for it. I earned it. I deserve it! It's not fair!!"

When I asked Jim how he had handled the news, he told me that he'd swallowed his anger for the moment in fear that he might blow up at his boss and lose his job. "I need the money," he said. "I have to work, but I'm sure not going to stay there. They don't deserve me."

Jim felt the three key factors that initiate stage-one anger: an experience that felt unfair and wrong, an inability to calmly remedy the situation, and an inability to either tolerate it or let it go.

⑾ Anne

Anne's parents had a history of heart problems, so when her doctor expressed some concern about her symptoms and recommended that she see a specialist, Anne made an appointment immediately. Knowing that doctors are sometimes late for appointments, she brought a book with her, thinking that she might have time to do some reading. Then she sat in the doctor's office, book in hand, while she waited—and waited, and waited—growing more impatient and indignant by the moment.

"I waited in her office for an hour and forty minutes," Anne complained. "It wouldn't matter if she were the best cardiologist in the country; that still wouldn't excuse her behavior. How could she keep me waiting that long? And then she didn't even apologize, didn't even acknowledge my wait!"

Like Jim, Anne believed that her experience was unfair, that she did not have any power since she needed the doctor's opinion and possibly her help. Anne also had the third key ingredient. She felt unable to simply tolerate what had happened or let it go. At least for a while, it bothered her.

Unlike Jim, Anne was not furious. She was indignant. She wanted and had expected that her time would be respected. At the very least, she had expected an explanation and a sincere apology.

⫴ Shelly

Shelly was annoyed. "I had a list of errands that just had to be done yesterday, and it just seemed like everything was against me. First, I left in a hurry and forgot the list. I had to drive back home to get it. Then I got to the store and couldn't find the three items I most needed to buy. I had to go to two different stores to track them down. On the way, I think I hit every red light in the city. Why is it that when I'm in a hurry and really need to get stuff done, life just doesn't cooperate?" she asked exasperatedly.

Like Jim and Anne, Shelly felt that her experience was unfair. She also acknowledged that she had no power over what items a store had in stock or when the city's traffic lights would turn green. And like Jim and Anne, she felt unable either to easily tolerate what happened or to simply let it go. While the intensity of her experience was much less than Jim's or Anne's, the three key factors that trigger anger were present here too.

Now that you know about these factors, you can notice them in your own experiences so that your own anger becomes less mysterious and more understandable and predictable. The exercise below is a way to begin.

EXERCISE: Identifying the Key Factors in Your Own Experience

Take a moment to think of an experience that made you angry, or work with your experience from the preceding exercise as you answer the following questions. You will use these answers in the next exercise, so be sure to write them down in your anger journal:

1. In what way did this particular event feel unfair, hurtful, or in some other way wrong?

2. What was it about the circumstances of this experience, or about yourself or the other person, that made you believe that you could not easily right the wrong?

3. What kept you from being able to either easily tolerate it or let the event go?

By answering these questions, you have most likely given yourself a better sense of the key triggering factors at work in your own experience. While this is useful information, there is more to learn here. In fact, these factors have a deeper significance that helps form the basis for using your anger as a guide to increasing your self-awareness in stage two.

The Deeper Significance of the Key Factors

If you're like many people, you believe that someone or something else, someone or something outside of you, causes your anger. After all, you are angry *with* someone or something, or you're concerned that someone is angry with you. Anger points a finger. It says, "That person is wrong"; "That situation is unfair"; "Something should not be." Or, if you are angry with yourself, your finger is pointed at you.

Either way, your anger focuses on someone or something that you feel is bad, someone or something unfair, something that you feel should not have happened. It's natural to believe that the person or situation that you have defined as bad or unfair caused your anger. Even though it may feel natural, however, that doesn't make it true. In fact, your anger is not caused by anyone or anything outside of you, bad or unfair though that person or situation may be.

The key factors that call forth your anger can be condensed into the following statement: *You become angry when you define reality as unacceptable and you feel unable to easily correct it, tolerate it, or let it go.* Stated this way, it becomes clearer that the reality of what has happened is not the key issue. What matters most is your judgment of your ability to handle this reality. It is your perception that causes you to become angry—your perception both that you are unable to accept the situation as it is and that, for whatever reason, you are unable to correct it in that moment.

This is a very human and understandable experience. Reality can be cruel and can feel overpowering. Your stage-one reaction of anger may seem—and actually be—the only way for you to get through the immediate situation. Used consciously and deliberately in stage two, though, when your immediate need for protection has passed, your anger can guide you to your own deep, vulnerable places. At that deep level, anger can help you strengthen as it increases your understanding, both of the situation and of yourself.

Your anger can help you accomplish these important tasks by leading you to the beliefs, feelings, and wounds that keep you from feeling able enough or powerful enough to either calmly work toward the change that you hope for or to accept that the upsetting reality is unchangeable and move on to thrive in your life in spite of it. Anger, used in stage two, can help set you free by showing you how to grow beyond the initially angering experience.

This in no way means that you should condone unacceptable behavior. It in no way means that the upsetting situation or experience is your fault. It does mean, however, that understanding your own anger and what it has to teach you in stage two is a major step toward resolving your inner pain, no matter what experience prompted it. This work is a major step toward handling the difficult relationship or working through the upsetting event, no matter who or what caused the problem. Increasing your understanding about your anger and its true cause is a pivotal step that will help you regain and even increase your sense of peace within yourself and with those around you. For now, you can move toward that understanding by reviewing the three key factors you explored in the last exercise so you can see their deeper significance at work in your own life.

EXERCISE:
Reviewing What Really Triggered Your Anger

As you review your former answers, do you notice that it wasn't the actual experience itself that caused your anger? Can you see that it was actually your belief that you were unable to calmly right this particular wrong, to accept it, or to let it go that resulted in your becoming angry? Take a moment now to write your observations in your journal.

If this is new information for you and you feel like you're struggling to make sense of it, don't worry. You will have many chances to revisit this information and you'll use it as part of the seven-step gift-of-anger process. It is this information that will begin to turn your anger into a healing and strengthening guide.

To further highlight the fact that becoming angry results from your belief about your capacity to handle the problem rather than the problem itself, take some time to think of a different experience. This time, recall an experience when others became angry but you remained calm. Perhaps this was a work experience or an experience with friends or family. What was it about the circumstances of this experience that enabled you to stay calm rather than needing the power boost of anger? Notice that either you believed you were equal to the task of solving this particular problem or you knew you would be able to tolerate the situation without feeling the need to change it. Either way, congratulate yourself for your capacity to handle this situation calmly, especially when others were unable to do so.

A Stage-One Loop

News reports from local to worldwide attest to the fact that it is far from common knowledge that anger has much more to do with someone's estimation of an event than it does with the event itself. In fact, rather than using anger as a guide to greater self-awareness and true empowerment, it seems a sadly common occurrence for people to stay in stage one, either moving from one angry experience to the next or reigniting their anger by reviewing the same experience over and over again. Both of these patterns are examples of what I call a *stage-one loop.*

Perhaps you, like so many of us, have been stuck in a stage-one loop. Here is one way this can happen. Not knowing how to work with and through your anger, you may have been stuffing it, acting it out, or just doing your best to get beyond it... until the next angering experience comes along. Cycling in and out of anger, you may feel stuck, not knowing what to do to break out of your angry behavior and move beyond it.

A variation of this unfortunate pattern occurs when you hang on to your anger as a way to express your refusal to condone someone else's bad behavior. Doing so, you cycle through your anger over and over again, each time you recall the other person's upsetting behavior. Like the negative loop I've described, this one doesn't work well either. Too often, the "someone else" does not care about or even notice the anger that you continually direct toward him or her. Even when the object of your anger is aware of it, the price of staying in a stage-one loop can be too high for you to healthfully bear. Essentially, you end up punishing yourself instead of the other person.

The Consequences of Remaining in a Stage-One Loop

Once you have faced the immediate situation, which may be over very quickly, your need for the protective power boost of your anger ends. At that point, unless you move to stage two and begin using your anger as a guide to increased self-awareness, you risk becoming stuck in a stage-one loop, with your anger continuing to vie for your attention by keeping you stressed and upset. Without moving to stage two, you cannot fully understand your experience. One way to think about this is that, as we will discuss further in the next two chapters, your anger will remain active until it serves its full purpose. That is, you are likely to reexperience this anger until you learn from it and then integrate what you've learned so that you have less need of a power boost in the future. Until then, your anger will keep causing you problems.

Physical problems. What kind of problems result from staying stuck in stage-one anger? You may feel it physically, as degrees of discomfort. If this discomfort is strong enough, you may find yourself saying such things as, "It's a pain in the neck"; "I want it off my back"; "I can't stomach this." In these cases, your unexamined anger becomes a physical stress factor.

There is much documented proof of the detrimental effects of physical stressors such as anger. Some possible effects include ulcers, colitis, irritable bowel syndrome, diarrhea, constipation, more frequent colds and flus, slower wound healing, a greater chance of serious infection, hardening of the arteries, heart attacks, type 2 diabetes, premenstrual syndrome, erectile dysfunction, and lowered libido (Hanson and Mendius 2009). Added to this list are headaches, backaches, allergic reactions, and high blood pressure (Jantz 1999). Also included are asthma and arthritis (Goleman 1995). The potential of having a stroke is the final addition to this partial list of physical consequences (Phillips 1998).

Mental, emotional, and spiritual problems. While the potential physical problems are impressive, they are not the whole story. There are also mental, emotional, and spiritual consequences to staying stuck in stage one. For instance, clients have repeatedly discussed the fact that prolonging stage one focuses your mind on divisive terms such as "good" versus "bad" or "me" versus "you." Thus, unexamined anger keeps you feeling and acting separate from other people. You cannot feel close to people if you do not trust them, so feeling connected, at one, or at peace with others is out of the question. "Ah," you may say, "but I do have people I trust." That may be true, but your mind will take you back to thoughts about the people you don't trust, and all too often, that is where your preoccupation will dwell.

Another problem caused by unexamined anger is that, having defined the other person as powerful enough to "cause" your anger, you are likely to feel less powerful as a result. You will have become a victim, stuck in a situation in which you believe someone or something else has power over your emotions—*making* you get angry. Your trust in others may be weakened, and quite possibly your trust in yourself as well.

Effects on mood and memories. Not only your mood, but also your memories may be affected. Studies have shown that you are much more likely to recall positive experiences when in a positive mood and negative experiences when feeling bad (Pert 1997). So, at the very least, remaining in stage one dampens your potential for joy. At worst, it may swallow you. Most of us have seen people like this. Their anger has become the center of their lives, and they have simply become angry people. No matter what the situation, they find a way to weave it into their anger story and use it as fuel to keep their story going.

At the other extreme are people who do not become intensely angry but are constantly irritated or annoyed. This may seem like a minor problem, or even just an everyday fact of life, but it is the accumulation of seemingly small annoyances that all too often pile up in our minds, leaving us little room for joy. It's not possible to focus on anger and focus on the beauty and positive possibilities around you simultaneously. You miss so much by remaining angry. Moving beyond anger may or may not be helpful to the person you're mad at, but it is crucial for your own well-being.

⑾ Ben

Ben was in his fifties. For this moderately successful dentist, work was his life. It was the one thing he felt really good at, so he worked long hours every day but Sundays. Ben had trouble showing even low levels of anger, let alone working through his upset feelings. He just wanted everyone to stay peaceful, including himself. So he tried to do whatever his wife asked, and he tried to shrug off any anger he felt toward family and friends. He did his best to act as if nothing was wrong and kept his anger at bay by overindulging in comfort food and wine. He was certain that if he just kept taking his mind off of his anger, it would go away. It was his second heart attack that changed his mind.

⑾ Lynn

Lynn was a workshop attendee who, told to pick a small angering experience, talked about her irritation with waiting in lines. "It never fails," she complained, "I always pick the slowest one. Guaranteed." As she explored her annoyance further, Lynn realized that she frequently felt irritated with life's pace. "Everything takes longer than I expect," she lamented. "It's not just the long lines. So often there are other complications— everything from needing help from people who are unavailable or don't get it right to my own need to take longer than I'd expected to get something done. It seems like I'm always in a hurry, always pushing to move faster, but feeling like I'm going slower." Thinking more deeply about her pace and the feelings that resulted from it, Lynn realized that she lived with a constant, low level of annoyance that flared into outright anger periodically. To some degree, Lynn was always angry.

Talking about the consequences of remaining angry, Lynn began to cry. "I have no idea what real joy feels like anymore," she said tearfully. "I can't even remember the last time I felt truly relaxed." Then, looking at the handout on the potential consequences of remaining angry, she added grimly, "Well, let's see. I'm going to a chiropractor now for my backache, and sometimes it seems like I never met a cold I didn't take home." Looking further down the list she continued, "Headaches for sure, and then there's high blood pressure. I just started taking medication for it last month." Looking up, she gave a defeated smile and said, "All right, I came to this workshop out of curiosity, but you've got my attention now."

EXERCISE:
A Checklist of Potential Consequences

Many clients who come to workshops or counseling minimize their anger at first, but staying in denial at any level just keeps you stuck. Painful though it may be, looking directly at your anger and how it may be affecting your life is a terrific motivator to make the changes you hoped for when you began reading this book. So I encourage you to take a look at the following partial list of potential consequences of staying in stage one. Then, complete the exercise that follows.

Notice the range of possible consequences from staying angry and check the ones that might apply to you:

Physical Consequences

☐ Allergic reactions

☐ Arthritis

☐ Asthma

☐ Backaches

☐ Colds

☐ Colitis

☐ Constipation

☐ Diarrhea

☐ Erectile dysfunction

☐ Flu

☐ Hardened arteries

☐ Headaches

☐ Heart attack

☐ High blood pressure

☐ Irritable bowel syndrome

☐ Lowered libido

☐ Premenstrual syndrome

☐ Serious infection

☐ Slower wound healing

☐ Stroke

☐ Ulcer

Mental Consequences

☐ Difficulty concentrating on daily tasks

☐ Divisiveness

☐ Impaired relationships

☐ Increased negative memories

☐ Lowered level of self-trust

☐ Mistrust of others

☐ Negative thinking

☐ Tendency to focus on angry thoughts

23

Emotional Consequences

☐ Alienation

☐ Anxiety

☐ Depression

☐ Feelings of inadequacy

☐ Feeling separate

☐ Less joy

☐ Lowered level of peace

☐ Negative mood

☐ Withdrawal

☐ _____

☐ _____

☐ _____

If you have issues that aren't on the list, add them on the blank lines I've included. Then, when you've finished checking those issues that apply to you and adding others, answer the following questions:

⦙⎸ How might resolving your anger affect you physically? Mentally? Emotionally? Spiritually?

⦙⎸ How might resolving your anger affect your level of self-esteem?

⦙⎸ What other changes might satisfactorily resolving your anger bring?

By answering the questions above, you're not only highlighting the problems your anger has caused you; you're also reminding yourself of some of the benefits that working with your anger in stage two can bring. Adding these answers to your anger journal, you can compare your sense of peace, self-esteem, and other changes that you may make as result of completing the upcoming process with those you hoped for in this exercise.

How Anger Prepares You for Stage Two

Clearly, remaining in stage one has a potentially high cost in terms of its ongoing effects on your physical, mental, emotional, and spiritual well-being. As you have seen in some of the examples in this chapter (and undoubtedly in your own life), anger frequently doesn't even bring the results you hoped for. Sometimes, perhaps too often, it brings you exactly the opposite. Anger does more than that, however; it also makes you uncomfortable, sometimes while you are angry and often afterwards, as we saw in the last exercise. And beyond these discomforts and ailments, anger can leave you feeling remorseful, sad, and lonely, wishing you could just take back your anger and redo the experience.

In addition to these repercussions from holding on to stage one, you will most likely pay a further price. Choosing not to examine and work through your anger, ultimately letting it go, puts you at risk for becoming more sensitive to the kind of situation that caused your angry reaction and more likely to become angry in reaction to similar experiences.

One way to think about these facts is that your stage-one anger is exacting this high price so that you will not want to stay there, so that you will want with all your heart to move beyond it to stage two. That is where your healing and growth awaits. In the next chapter, you will see what gives your anger this positive potential.

CHAPTER 2

The Power of Stage Two

Whether it lasted for a few seconds, a few minutes, or longer, you have come through your angering experience. Now you have an opportunity to use that experience to expand your self-awareness and increase your sense of personal power. How do you do this? By moving to stage two. Here is where your anger can help you uncover and heal emotional pain. Here is where it can help you expand your awareness and increase your capacity to calmly and successfully handle whatever life brings you.

While the upcoming chapters explaining the gift-of-anger process will help you understand and navigate stage two, this chapter will explore the attributes of anger that form the foundation for understanding it as a two-stage emotion and using it in a vitally positive way in this second stage.

Attribute One: Anger Is Normal

The first attribute of anger seems so obvious that it's often overlooked: anger is normal. Not only do *you* feel anger, but everyone else feels it too. Usually when I say this, clients will respond with "Of course." It seems obvious that we all feel anger at times. Yet how many people do you know who say, "Oh, I'm angry. That's okay. It's normal." In fact, you probably don't know anyone who says that. You may, however, know people who say, "I'm angry and it's someone else's fault!" Perhaps you know other people who say, "I'm angry. How can I get even with the other person?" You might even know people who say, "I'm angry! How can I hide it? I have to hide it because good people don't get angry (or God-fearing people don't get angry, or I shouldn't be angry because I'm supposed to more enlightened than that)".

There are many ways to think about anger; but only when you think of it as normal—and therefore potentially useful—will you take the time to really explore and understand your anger. Acknowledging the universality and potential usefulness of anger opens the doorway to becoming curious about your particular experience and exploring it deeply to see what it has to teach you.

Attribute Two: Anger Covers Painful Feelings

As you explore your anger, you might notice that it covers other feelings. These are vulnerable feelings and often painful. They are the upsetting feelings that make you feel smaller and weaker, and thus in need of the power boost that anger brings.

A Sample of Painful Feelings

In the earlier example of my experience in an isolated office, I felt afraid and helpless underneath my anger. Jim, who was passed over for a promotion, felt betrayed and rejected. Anne, waiting impatiently in her doctor's office, said that she felt devalued. Steve, chasing another car, said he felt powerless. Ben, who had two heart attacks before being willing to work with his anger, said he felt inadequate and ashamed. Shelly, trying to get her errands done quickly, said she felt overwhelmed. Carolyn, needing a break from caring for her mother, said she felt taken for granted and unfairly treated.

Think of the last time you were mad. What else were you feeling? The list in the following exercise is by no means complete, but it is an indication of how numerous and how painful these underlying emotions can be. Use it to help identify what is usually masked by your anger. As you complete the exercise, notice the feelings most commonly present in your own life.

EXERCISE: A Checklist of Painful Feelings

With a past angering experience in mind, complete the following:

1. Review the partial list of feelings that follows and place a checkmark by those that you either recall feeling repeatedly or that elicit a strong response from you as you read them.

2. Add any feelings that seem to fit for you but are not on this list.

- ☐ Abandoned
- ☐ Afraid
- ☐ Ashamed
- ☐ Belittled
- ☐ Betrayed
- ☐ Blamed
- ☐ Controlled
- ☐ Criticized
- ☐ Disrespected
- ☐ Made helpless
- ☐ Humiliated
- ☐ Hurt
- ☐ Ignored
- ☐ Impatient
- ☐ Inadequate
- ☐ Invisible

☐ Manipulated

☐ Overpowered

☐ Overwhelmed

☐ Rejected

☐ Shamed

☐ Slighted

☐ Unappreciated

☐ Unfairly treated

☐ Taken for granted

☐ Vulnerable

☐ _____

☐ _____

☐ _____

3. Look at the feelings you've checked and rank them in order of their intensity in your life, with 1 being the most prevalent.

Now that you have identified one or more feelings underlying your anger, include them in your journal. Then you can explore how these feelings summon the power boost of your anger.

How These Feelings Trigger Anger

Each of the feelings on the checklist can be extremely distressing and can diminish anyone's sense of personal power. Furthermore, everyone experiences at least some of them some of the time. When experiencing one or more of them makes you feel too vulnerable, too much at the mercy of someone or something else, you're likely to interpret this experience as wrong or unfair, beyond your power to calmly correct, and more than you can either easily accept or let go—the key factors that trigger anger. With this interpretation, you will probably react automatically with the power boost that anger brings.

The fact is that when we feel strong, secure, and confident, we are usually able to accept the reality of a situation and decide how best to respond to it. We may not like the situation. We may even dislike it intensely and commit to changing it, if that's at all possible. But we do not need to become angry. We become angry only when our underlying feelings make us so vulnerable that we see the person or situation we're facing as not only unacceptable but also too powerful to face without the protective power boost that anger provides.

Depending on the level of your sensitivity to your underlying feelings, you may have learned to cover those hurtful emotions with your anger so quickly and automatically that you haven't yet realized that the feelings are even there. Instead, your attention may immediately focus on the object of your anger rather than on what you are experiencing underneath your power boost. If so, the gift-of-anger process will help you to recognize and understand your own painful emotions. The process will also help you explore what causes them and how to heal them. How can this be possible? The next attribute of anger is part of the answer.

Attribute Three: Anger Is Uniquely Personal

You've probably noticed that the same situation can make one person angry while another person feels only mildly annoyed and a third person feels neutral. In fact, each of us experiences anger in our own individual way.

Loretta, for example, is an older woman who became angry when she felt ignored by her friend during a party they both attended. Loretta reacted with silence and retreat, experiencing her anger privately. Safely alone, she continually replayed her experience, her anger growing more firmly established with each replay.

Another person, finding himself or herself in Loretta's situation, might have been openly angry with the friend. Someone else might have presumed that the friend had a good reason for seeming to ignore her, even though that reason was as yet unknown. Still another might have responded with concern and immediately asked the friend if anything was wrong. Four different people with four distinct reactions—each with their own unique anger pattern, differing both in the degree to which they experienced anger and their manner of expression.

You can think of anger as an *emotional fingerprint*. Just as each person has his or her own unique, physical fingerprint, so we each have our own unique anger pattern. Your pattern may overlap with someone else's, but it won't be exactly the same. This fact makes your anger useful because your pattern has a lot to tell you about yourself. As a uniquely personal emotional fingerprint, it has information geared solely to you.

EXERCISE:
Exploring Your Unique Anger Pattern

To explore your own anger pattern, you might keep an anger diary for the next week. You can make entries in your anger journal so that all of your discoveries are in one place. Here is how to do so:

1. Write down the time of day and a brief description of the circumstances each time you become angry.

2. Label the intensity level of your anger using one of the descriptors below or writing in your own:

Mild annoyance	Anger
Irritation	Fury
Exasperation	Rage
Resentment	Other _____
Frustration	

3. Note any vulnerable feelings that come up along with or just underneath your anger. The list in the previous exercise will help you identify them.

4. Keep track of how long you stay angry in each situation.

5. After keeping your diary for a week, review it to notice:

    a. What kind of experiences elicited your anger? How are they similar to each other? How are they different from each other?

    b. How angry did you usually become? Did your anger cover a range of intensity or did you usually experience the same or near-same intensity level? Did you stay angry for a few minutes? A few days? The entire week?

    c. What vulnerable feeling or feelings did you notice along with your anger? Which did you notice the most frequently?

    d. What else do you notice about your particular experience of anger?

Your anger diary will help you understand your unique anger pattern more deeply and thoroughly, giving you new information about what kind or kinds of experiences are, at present, too hard for you to handle without the power boost that your anger brings. You can use this information when you follow the upcoming seven-step process, checking your progress against what you've written in this initial period.

Attribute Four: Anger Is Based on Personal History

What differs for each of us and determines our individual anger patterns is the set of beliefs each of us has learned from the experiences that formed our personal histories. So, let's say that you were raised in a family of people who loved you, helped you build your self-confidence, and treated you and others kindly. In that case, the beliefs you learned might include believing that you can trust your feelings. You might also believe that there is value in helping others when they are upset or angry. Conversely, if you were raised in an abusive household, you might distrust your emotions and those of other people. You might also believe that when others are angry, it's either time to back away and protect yourself or time to become angry in return. You could even believe that another's anger requires you to make sure that your anger is more powerful than theirs.

While the above example is extreme, it makes the point that you, like everyone else, have your own beliefs about yourself and your world, and these beliefs are based on what you've learned from your unique past. In chapter 3 you'll learn how these beliefs formed as a result of your personal history. You'll also be exploring further how they're linked to your feelings and to your responses to each of your current experiences, including those to which you react with anger. The painful feelings that cause you to interpret a current experience as wrong or unfair, beyond your power to calmly correct, and more than you can accept—the key factors that trigger anger—are connected to your beliefs.

Personal Beliefs You Learned as a Child

While you can form a belief at any time, you most likely learned some of your most basic and influential convictions from your parents and other authority figures when you were very young—too young to realistically evaluate what you were learning. By the time you were old enough to accurately analyze these beliefs, you might not have even thought of evaluating them because you had already accepted them as true. They had already become part of your accepted frame of reference, helping you to define and understand yourself and to interpret the world around you. As a result, some of your assumptions about your abilities and your limitations and about how the world should and should not be come from beliefs you formed in your distant past.

If you are like most people, some of those beliefs learned so early in your life were inaccurate. Other beliefs that may have been accurate once are now outdated. After all, you're grown now and your circumstances have changed significantly. So, like everyone else, along with many beliefs that are true, you also hold convictions that were either never accurate or are now outdated.

⫯⫯ Maggie

Maggie, whose mother was an alcoholic, learned very early in life that her job was to take care of her mom. She learned to put her own needs second, and even as a young adult she continued to take care of others and be dutiful rather than taking time to focus on her own wishes—or even really know what those wishes might be. Maggie's anger emerged in the form of resentments, which she held onto and mulled over periodically. Until she began exploring her anger, Maggie didn't realize the significance of the fact that her mother also held onto resentments rather than working through them, as did her grandmother. Now Maggie understands that holding onto resentments is part of a pattern that she learned, just as her mother learned it and, quite possibly, her grandmother as well.

Maggie is representative of many adults whose parents, because of their own unresolved issues and their own mistaken beliefs, were unable to parent their children well. As a result, Maggie grew into adulthood with very limiting beliefs about who she was and who she was allowed to become—beliefs that typically remain years or even a lifetime after a child has grown to adulthood and possibly left the abusive situation.

Of course, most parents are not alcoholics or abusive, and so very many adults did not have abusive parents. There are countless examples of caring parents who meant only the best for their children; yet, being human, these parents still had limiting beliefs that may have kept them from seeing and responding to at least some of their children's needs. In addition, there are countless adults who, as children, may have misinterpreted their parents' statements or actions and still hold inaccurate beliefs as a result.

⫯⫯ Bill

Bill recalled that he had loved to play the piano as a child. Repeatedly told how talented he was and continually asked to perform for family members and their friends, Bill interpreted those requests to mean that in order to gain love you had to be entertaining. You had to perform. Bill's belief that he could not just be himself and still be loved eventually resulted in his refusal to continue playing the instrument he had so enjoyed. He is working with his anger now, though, and his awareness has grown as a result. In fact, he now recalls incidents that have convinced him that his parents felt insecure about their own worth and performed to be included and to gain love, just like he did.

Bill also acknowledges now that his parents most likely meant well and probably thought they were helping him to build his confidence by complimenting him and asking him to perform for them. However, it's all too easy for children to believe that they are not really loved just for themselves alone, and all too easy for parents to miss the signs of an insecure child. After all, every parent had his or her own difficult childhood. Each parent has his or her own incorrect beliefs, and his or her own potential feelings of lack of love and acceptance.

Of course, parents aren't the only ones who influence children. Grandparents, aunts, uncles, teachers, and even other children—in fact, any authority figure in a child's life—can be the source of a limiting belief.

Maggie and Bill have corrected some of their limiting beliefs so that they now see themselves, their experiences, and their potential more clearly and fully. As a result, they have come to feel more powerful than they used to, not through the power boost of their anger but because their understanding of both themselves and of those around them has grown. Like Maggie and Bill, you hold beliefs about yourself and your world that are inaccurate. *We all do.* As a result, your anger emerges in stage one as protective energy and can be used in stage two to help you see yourself and the world around you ever more clearly. With this clarity comes more peaceful and successful action.

EXERCISE: The Historical Basis of Your Anger

In my clinical experience, I've noticed that many people have been surprised by the idea that when and how they become angry is usually learned behavior. If you, like so many others, are used to accepting (or rejecting) your anger without deeply considering its origin, answering the following questions may help you to see your anger, and perhaps some of your beliefs, in a new light. Again, record your answers in your journal so that you have a record that you can review later on, as you complete the seven steps:

1. What behaviors or lack of behavior did you fear might make your parents or other authority figures in your early life angry or cause them to withdraw their love? What actions did you limit and what behaviors did you increase as a result? What did you believe about them and their love for you as a result? What did you believe about yourself? What do you believe now?

2. Make a list of what used to make you angry as a child. Then, make another list of what makes you angry now. Compare your lists and notice how you have changed, and also notice what remains the same. Is there anything on your list that you know would be on either parent's list as well? Anything that would be on a grandparent's list or the list of any other authority figure in your early life?

3. How was anger handled in your family? Who was allowed to become angry, and how were they allowed to show it? Who, if anyone, allowed you to become angry, and how were you allowed to show it? If you weren't allowed to show it, what did you do instead? What do you do now?

Answering the questions above has likely given you information about the historical basis of your own anger. You've probably also gained some insight into what in your past contributed to some of your current beliefs about anger, about yourself, and about the world around you. This is an important exploration that will continue throughout the book. However, your personal history and the beliefs it engendered aren't the only important influences in your life. Like everyone else, you are also influenced by the beliefs that permeate our culture.

Cultural Beliefs

While the beliefs I described in the examples above were formed as a result of each person's individual history, as a culture we also have widely held beliefs, formed as a result of our shared history. To the extent that these culturally accepted beliefs are incorrect, they limit our ability to see ourselves clearly and interpret the world around us accurately.

One well-known cultural belief that limits our ability to see clearly and fully is the belief that life should be fair. This belief gets expressed in many different ways: "If I work diligently and hard, then I will reach my goal"; "If I'm nice to you, then you'll be nice to me"; "If I'm a good person, then only good things will happen to me."

This conviction, in all of its many forms, is so very understandable. It's a belief we *want* to be true, one we want to be able to trust. In fact, there are a number of books that owe their popularity to this premise—the idea that you can guarantee an outcome if you behave in a certain way. Unfortunately, this popular and enticing belief is an exaggeration of the truth. While you can certainly work to gain a specific outcome and often reach your goal, no one can guarantee its realization. People are usually kind. Hard work does usually pay off. If you are nice to someone, they are usually nice back. Usually, but not always.

The fact that life is not necessarily fair and that no one can guarantee that it will be can be a hard lesson to learn. Living includes the incredible joy of feeling in charge of your destiny when your life is going well and the feelings of helplessness that arise when you realize how unfair life can sometimes be and how little control you may actually have over particular situations.

Like most people, you may want to be in charge, to have things go your way. You may have even been taught that having things go your way is a measure of how successful you are, how correctly you are living your life. When problems happen (as they often do), you may blame yourself as well as others. If something truly harmful happens to you, you may find yourself feeling outraged. *Why me? It isn't fair! I did everything right!* And along with your outrage at the other person or situation, you may be angry with yourself, too. Consider the example of Andrea.

⑈ Andrea

In Andrea's case, doing everything right meant eating a healthful diet, meditating, and exercising daily. It meant getting regular medical checkups. "Right" meant being a loving wife and mother and volunteering her time at her youngest daughter's preschool. It meant attending religious services each week. Andrea did everything right. And then she got breast cancer.

"I think we got it in time," the doctor said after the lumpectomy. Then he discussed the chemotherapy treatments, the course of radiation, and the use of tamoxifen, "just to be sure."

Andrea took it all in stride until the second chemotherapy treatment and the seemingly endless vomiting, headaches, and clumps of hair on her pillow that followed. Then she became enraged. She was angry at the cancer for invading her body, angry with God for allowing it to happen, and, most of all, angry with herself for not being more in control of her life. "I don't know what I could have done," she sobbed, "but whatever it is, I should have done it. This just shouldn't have happened!"

Eventually, after much work moving through stage two of her anger, Andrea was able to accept the reality of her situation and work with it. "I realize that it's not about fairness or blame," she said. "I did everything I could. I still do. And I know that the things I do can help me stay well and have the kind of life I want, but they can't guarantee it."

Andrea learned other valuable lessons as well. Rather than struggling to take control and make things happen the way she wanted them to, she learned to relax and appreciate what is here right now. Free of cancer for a year now, she says, "I do what I can for the future, but I'm more in the moment now, not so worried about what might happen. I'm grateful for each experience."

So many of the inaccurate cultural beliefs that cause us pain and anger have to do with *shoulds*. "Life should be fair, and so it will be." "Others should believe as I do, and so they will." "He or she should behave a certain way because that's how I would behave." We make these statements to ourselves automatically, often not even realizing that we're making them and that, at least in the moment, we believe them and expect them to happen. While it's terrific when they do happen, reality is not always cooperative; nor are we always as able to control reality as we might wish.

To the extent that we count on our beliefs rather than leaving room for the unexpected to happen, we hold ourselves open for disappointment and disillusionment when reality doesn't live up to our expectations. We experience painful feelings that result in interpreting the experience as wrong or unfair, beyond our power to calmly correct, and more than we can accept or let go. Anger is the result, triggered as a protective power boost in stage one and then available to help us strengthen and grow beyond our limiting expectations in stage two.

EXERCISE: Identifying Your Cultural Beliefs

The list below contains a number of beliefs widely held in our culture. You undoubtedly have heard them and likely accept at least some of them. You may not be used to seeing them written down, though, and they may seem simplistic and not really believable as you read them. Even so, I encourage you to acknowledge the ones you hope for. Place a check mark by each of those and add any others that are important to you. By doing so, you will give yourself a fuller picture of the beliefs that guide your expectations. Record your findings in your journal.

☐ Life should be fair. If it isn't, something is wrong.

☐ The good will be rewarded.

☐ The bad will be punished.

☐ If I work diligently and hard, then I will reach my goal.

☐ You have to earn your results.

☐ People should obey the rules.

☐ If I'm nice to you, then you'll be nice to me.

☐ If I'm a good person, then only good things will happen to me.

☐ _____

☐ _____

☐ _____

Some people have completed this exercise without checking any cultural beliefs. Others have checked many. Simply notice what you have checked and then see if you can more easily recognize those beliefs as they come up in your life. When you do note these beliefs in operation, check in to determine how often they lead to anger if the unexpected happens and reality does not conform to your hopes.

Attribute Five: Anger Offers the Potential for Change

While almost all of us have held onto beliefs that keep us reacting over and over again in the same way, each time lessening our ability to be fully present in the moment, many of us have made healthy changes as well. As we have each grown and learned more about ourselves and about the world around us, many of us have healed the causes of some of our painful feelings. We have altered our beliefs and retrained ourselves in new, more realistic, and personally satisfying ways. So, if you are like many other people, you can remember situations that used to make you angry but no longer do. This fact, that each of us can alter our anger pattern as a result of our own emerging awareness and growth, is the fifth characteristic of anger.

⑾ Jenny

Jenny spoke of how often she had become angry in her first job. A young administrative assistant at a busy marketing firm, she had constantly felt overloaded at work. Finally, in anger and desperation, she had decided to find another job. Though there was much about her work that she loved, she simply couldn't take the stress any longer.

Jenny had secured a new position and was preparing to give her notice when she began to realize how much about her present situation she actually liked. When overwhelmed and at the end of her rope, it was easy to overlook positive aspects of her job. But, with a little space, she began to understand what she would be giving up. Jenny remembered that she liked the company's mission and appreciated the potential for advancement offered there. She thought about her coworkers, some of whom had become friends. She would miss seeing them daily if she left.

As a result, Jenny hesitantly sat down with her boss and explained her problem. After the meeting, she emerged from her boss's office with her work prioritized so that she knew what to do and in what order and what to put aside if she ran out of time. She also emerged with a new awareness of how valued she was at her present company.

As a child, Jenny had been taught the importance of doing tasks thoroughly, quickly, and well. In my office, she explained that her mother would show her how to do something once, telling Jenny to pay attention so she could do it correctly by herself. Jenny said that she sensed her mother's disappointment whenever she asked for further help and felt ashamed for needing assistance. As a result, Jenny came to believe that she should always be able to produce high-quality work, no matter what the circumstances, and that she should be able to handle whatever came her way without asking for help. "I didn't really expect anything positive to come from talking with my boss," she explained to me. "It never did when I was growing up. I just so wanted to keep my job and couldn't figure out anything else to do. Now that I've talked to my boss, I don't get angry so readily or give up so easily at work," she said. "Instead, I know to ask for help. I know I may not always get it, but now l know it's worth a try."

ılı Rick

When Rick was growing up, his parents called him stupid whenever he made a mistake. "For years I thought I really was stupid, and I got mad at anyone who reminded me of how dumb I was by calling me names. But then I noticed that I was always getting honors in school. You can't get the grades I got and be stupid."

What Rick eventually realized is that, although his parents chose an unfortunately hurtful method, they were actually trying to motivate him to do his best. Now when someone calls him a name, he doesn't automatically react with anger. Instead, he reminds himself that name-calling is a sign of the other person's limitations and does not need to become his problem, too. Instead of taking it personally, Rick now asks what the real problem is.

EXERCISE: Tracking Your Own Change

Take a moment to think about how the focus or extent of your own anger may have changed, and then, using your journal, answer the following:

1. What used to make you angry that either no longer does or makes you less angry now? Can you trace that process and explain how the change happened? How have your beliefs altered in this area? How have your beliefs about yourself changed?

2. Reviewing your life, what other changes have you made that are most noticeable and important to you? How are your beliefs

different now in these areas? How are your beliefs about yourself different?

3. What of your own personal anger pattern would you like to change now? What beliefs about yourself would you like to be different?

Many of us can recall experiences that awakened new awareness and resulted in a diminishment of the frequency or extent of our anger. It's also true that you don't have to wait for chance events to help you correct mistaken beliefs. You can consciously change your anger pattern, as many already have. The gift-of-anger process is based on this ability.

We all experience emotions that, in great part, are a natural outgrowth of our earlier experiences and the beliefs and expectations they engendered. No matter what the present-day situation is, we can only view it through the lens of those limiting convictions. As a result, our response to any situation is constricted by the potentially inaccurate, historically based beliefs that we hold. We limit ourselves this way unless and until we bring greater clarity and accuracy to our understanding of the current situation. This is the purpose of the seven-step process that you will explore and work with, beginning in chapter 4.

Reality may well be unfair. You may have been treated in ways that felt—and were—horribly cruel. No matter what the circumstances, though, the most reliably successful way to deal with these experiences is to update your own beliefs so that you can see both your current situation and yourself as accurately as possible. Doing so will give you the most flexibility to find a workable solution and the greatest opportunity to thrive in your life in spite of the difficulties life may bring.

You are designed for growth. You are designed to take your experiences and distill information from them that will increase your consciousness. You are designed to widen and clarify your ability to clearly see and to respond to life positively. By continuing to set yourself free from limiting or outgrown beliefs about yourself and your world, you can adapt to life's changing reality and move toward an ever-more-aware state of understanding, equanimity, and compassion. This is your potential as a human being and your opportunity, as well.

CHAPTER 3

The Nature of Beliefs and Feelings

In chapter 2 you learned that painful feelings often trigger your anger and that your beliefs and your feelings are linked. A solid understanding of this link, as well as an understanding of the origins of your beliefs and feelings, will greatly facilitate your work with the gift-of-anger process. In this chapter, you'll learn about the link in greater detail and we'll examine how you formed many of your beliefs, how they affect your feelings, and the conscious choices you can make to update your beliefs and change the way you feel.

The Feelings Formula

Like many people, you may have been taught that your feelings are beyond your control and are simply a natural part of who you are. But actually, that's not quite true. While your capacity for a certain feeling is innate, most often your particular response to a situation is learned. Your unconscious, automatic choice of feelings in response to a particular situation is usually a natural outgrowth of your prior training and the beliefs it led you to establish. In other words, what you feel in response to a particular situation is often guided by your beliefs. Years ago, a psychologist named Albert Ellis (Ellis and Harper 1997) devised a formula to explain this fact. His formula was simple: A + B = C.

A is the *activating experience*, the actual situation or experience that occurred. B stands for your *belief system*, your established beliefs, attitudes, habits, values, and expectations. C stands for the *consequences*, which are your emotions and behavior that resulted from your actual experience being modified by your preexisting beliefs. Simply put, when something happens (A), your beliefs about the event (B) will determine how you feel and what you do (C). Here are some examples.

⑪ Matt

Matt started a new diet and exercise program to counter his growing weight and increasing shortness of breath. On the fourth day of his new regime his boss called him in, angry at his performance with a client (A). Matt had learned to blame others for his difficulties and to comfort himself with food (B). On his way home, Matt grumbled resentfully to himself about his boss's unfairness and then stopped off at the store for his favorite snacks (C).

Having learned to define himself as the injured party and to blame others for whatever went wrong, Matt's ingrained beliefs kept him from realizing that his boss might have had a valid point to make about Matt's handling of his client. His beliefs also kept him from considering that this experience might have provided an opportunity to learn to do his job more successfully and, ultimately, help him feel better about himself. Instead, his established beliefs led him to conclude that he was a victim in need of comfort. This dynamic meant that temporary comfort is all that he gave to himself. Real comfort came only after his anger caused him enough problems to compel him to explore his feelings and his beliefs more deeply.

⑾ Madeline

Madeline sat waiting, yet again, for her consistently late friend (A). Madeline was intimidated by confrontation and believed that she would be unable to calmly talk with her friend and successfully negotiate a firm meeting time (B). Madeline could feel her frustration level rise with each passing minute, but she did her best to suppress it so she wouldn't risk a confrontation when her friend finally showed up (C).

Like many people, rather than learning how to stand up for herself, Madeline had learned to avoid confrontation whenever possible. Since she liked her friend and felt unable to successfully talk with her about her lateness, Madeline felt powerless to get her need for punctuality met. By feeling unable to ask for what she wanted, she gave her friend all the power to decide their true meeting time and then felt frustrated as a result. She did so until her frustration finally pushed her to tell her friend how she felt.

⑾ Evelyn

Evelyn offers a final example, one that shows how complicated the A + B = C formula can become when we interact with each other. Strong and self-reliant, Evelyn managed a difficult job while caring for her family as well. Recently she had persuaded her elderly father to move in with her and her family so she could ensure that he received the care he needed. But shortly after he arrived at Evelyn's home, his condition took a turn for the worse. So instead of getting comfort at Evelyn's house, her dad was lying in pain in a hospital, and no one knew why.

Evelyn felt protective of her dad and concerned at his seeming frailty. Her father, on the other hand, had always acted strong and in charge, and he was determined to continue to do so even in his currently weakened condition.

As the doctor began listing diseases that might be a possible cause for her dad's symptoms, Evelyn felt her concern for her father escalate. Wanting to protect her dad from a potentially devastating diagnosis, she immediately told the doctor not to talk about this now. Evelyn's father, wanting to remain strong and in charge, responded angrily to Evelyn, telling her to behave more respectfully to the doctor. At his words, Evelyn seemed to shrink a bit. She closed her mouth and didn't say another word.

Later, when she and I discussed what had happened, Evelyn was struck by her response to her father's reprimand. Even though she was an adult with kids of her own, and even though she had assumed responsibility for her father's care, Evelyn realized that as soon as her father reprimanded her, she felt and reacted like a small child. "I've always wanted him to be proud of me, always tried to please him. Even now, I still do," she said, chagrined. "I felt ashamed that I made him angry, and at the same time I felt angry at him for not appreciating my efforts. These are the same reactions I've always had."

There are several A + B = C examples in Evelyn's story, as there are in many of our daily interactions with people:

1. Evelyn's reaction to the doctor is one example. Hearing the possible diagnoses (A) filtered by her belief that hearing them might make her dad feel worse (B), Evelyn reacted protectively by directing the doctor not to tell her father about possible diseases that he might have (C).

2. Evelyn's father's reaction to her is another A + B = C example. When Evelyn spoke out to the doctor (A), her father heard her words through the filter of his own limiting belief that even now he should be strong and in control (B). He reacted angrily by reprimanding his daughter and felt more powerful by doing so (C).

3. Evelyn's reaction to her father is a third example. Her father had always been the authority, and winning his respect had been, and still was, a paramount desire of Evelyn's. When he reprimanded her (A), she heard his words filtered by her belief that once again she had tried her best and still failed to please

him (B), and she felt ashamed and unappreciated (C), just as she always had when growing up.

Evelyn's experience exemplifies how complex Ellis's formula can be when applied to real life. Something happens (A), and it is interpreted differently by each person involved, with meaning filtered through and limited by each person's set of beliefs (B). Then everyone involved responds with feelings and behaviors appropriate to each one's limited interpretation of what happened (C). All the while, each person believes that they are seeing the situation objectively, accurately, and fully and is convinced that they're responding to it appropriately. Of course, each person may also believe that anyone who interprets and/or responds to the situation differently is wrong.

EXERCISE: Using the Feelings Formula

Now that you've read a variety of examples, take a look at how *you* act out the feelings formula, by recalling one of your own angering experiences. You can choose an experience in which you know only your side of the formula, but if possible, choose one that you later resolved so that you can discuss the other person's use of the formula as well. The example included with the questions will show you how. If you know only your side of the formula, answer questions 1 through 3 only. If you know the other person's use of the formula, you can answer all of the questions. To keep this from becoming too complicated, use an experience that didn't involve more than one other person.

When you have your experience in mind, complete the following:

1. Factually, without interpretation, state what happened. (Example: My friend cancelled a trip with me at the last minute.)

2. How did you interpret what happened? (Example: I told myself that he did not want to go because he didn't really care about me.)

3. What resulting emotions did you feel along with anger? (Example: I felt hurt, lonely, and unappreciated.)

4. When you talked with the other person to resolve the issue, what did the other person say happened? (Example: He admitted that he had lost a client and didn't have the money to go on the trip.)

5. What was the other person's interpretation of what happened? (Example: He was afraid that if he told me why he had to cancel our trip, I would think he wasn't good at his job and would think less of him.)

6. What resulting emotions did the other person feel? (Example: He said he felt embarrassed and fearful of being belittled.)

7. How did you feel and behave when you learned the truth? (Example: I felt relieved that I wasn't the reason he cancelled, and I felt sympathetic toward his feelings and his fears. I told him that I understood and appreciated knowing the truth and that I wanted us to be able to be honest with each other, even when doing so was difficult or potentially painful.)

We all frequently follow the A + B = C formula. We all respond emotionally and behave in ways that in great part are a natural outgrowth of our earlier experiences and the beliefs they engendered. No matter what the present-day situation is, our response is guided and limited by beliefs about ourselves and about the world that we may have established many years ago.

That's a lot of power for your beliefs to have—the power to define your view of reality and your response to it. To the extent that your beliefs are accurate, it is power well placed. To the extent that your beliefs are inaccurate, as were those of the people in these examples, it is misplaced power and an opportunity for growth in stage two.

Where do they come from, these powerful, limiting beliefs about ourselves and the world that sometimes turn out to be as incorrect as they are fervently held? Like Ellis's formula for the creation of feelings, there is a formula for the creation of beliefs.

Creating and Maintaining Your Beliefs

In great part, you form and maintain your beliefs according to four simple rules. While we all use these rules much of the time, most of us do so automatically. In fact, just as you may remain unaware that you're either using these rules or forming a belief as a result of them, you may even be unaware that they exist. This fact makes these very simple rules especially powerful.

These four rules often govern the establishment of your view of yourself and of those around you, a view that is usually both formed and constricted by your beliefs. These rules also help keep your views in place, so that you continue to see only what you expect to see. They work to help you form a positive belief, guiding you in deciding what you like or want. They also help you form a negative belief, leading you to conclude that you don't like a particular item or do not want a particular event to occur. Most important, these four simple rules, when applied consciously, can help you to see more of reality. By using the four rules to update your beliefs, you'll be better able to see issues, experiences, and people more clearly and accurately, just like Matt, Madeline, and Evelyn learned to do.

Here are the four rules:

1. **Rule One: State It.** State something as absolute fact. State it unequivocally, leaving no room for doubt.

2. **Rule Two: Believe It.** When stating it, act as if you truly believe it. You do not actually need to believe what you're asserting. You simply need to be the best actor or actress you can be.

3. **Rule Three: Feel It.** Make your statement as emotionally powerful as you can. Boost its power by evoking as many of the five senses (sight, smell, taste, touch, hearing) as possible.

4. **Rule Four: Repeat It.** Repeat this process often.

I learned these rules when I started using hypnosis as a therapeutic tool to help my clients. Most people who use hypnosis learn some version of these rules, but they are not the only ones to use them. You can also see the rules playing out in most advertisements, since ads are designed to form or alter your beliefs so that you will prefer a specific product. Think about some of the advertisements you've seen recently. Here is what happens in them:

1. The person in the commercial tells you that the product is absolutely, wonderfully perfect. (*Rule one is to state something as absolute fact.*)

2. Because the people in the advertisement are being paid to tell you this, they are doing the best acting job possible in order to make you believe it. (*Rule two is to act as if you truly believe what you're saying.*)

3. The actors or actresses use all of their senses and, by implication, invite you to do the same. In the ad, they happily use the product so that you can *see* them doing so. They tell you how wonderful it is so that you can *hear* about its incredible value. They use the product successfully, inviting you, via imagination, to *feel* yourself doing the same. And, if it is something to *smell* or *taste*, they do so rapturously. (*Rule three is to boost the power of your statement by evoking as many of the five senses as possible.*)

4. Advertisers seek to bring you their ads as often as possible. If you are watching a television show, you may well see the same ad more than once. If you watch a number of shows, you may see the same ad a number of times. (*Rule four is to repeat this process often.*)

Now that you've explored the four rules, the following exercise will help you practice discerning them in the advertisements you see.

EXERCISE:
Unpacking a Television or Magazine Ad

Now that you know the rules to create a belief, try noticing how they are applied in a television or magazine ad. To identify the rules most easily, pick an advertisement for food and then notice what the person in the ad says and does to try to make you want the product. Then:

1. Notice the unequivocally positive statements about the product. (*rule one*)

2. Identify what is said or done to convince you that the person featured believes what he or she is saying and that you should too. (*rule two*)

3. Pay attention to how he or she engages your emotions and as many of your five senses as possible. (*rule three*)

4. If you are watching television, count how many times you see the same ad in an evening or a week. (*rule four*)

When you have done this exercise for yourself, you can have fun with it by watching a variety of ads with your family or with friends. You can make a game of it by seeing who can most quickly notice how the rules are used in different advertisements. Then, have everyone rate the advertisements according to how effective you each think they are, and explain why.

While you can have fun doing this exercise, it can also be serious training for picking apart a belief and deepening your understanding of what makes you personally accept or reject that belief. Do this exercise a few times and you may find yourself more automatically questioning what you have been taught to believe and whether what others say is true or false. The more you practice with these rules, the more you'll notice the application of these rules in your personal life.

Applying the Rules to Your Life

Are these rules applicable to your life? Completing the exercise above probably convinced you that the four rules are operating in advertisements, but do they truly work in everyday situations? Do they really help you form your beliefs, and can they truly help you to update them? The simple answer is yes. These four rules form the basis for how you developed your beliefs about yourself and about those around you, sometimes at a very early age. They are also the foundation for how you maintain your beliefs now and how you can change them if you wish.

What you were told emphatically, either in the distant past or more recently, by authorities who believed what they were saying (rule one), and what you accepted as truth (two), either because you were too young to dispute it or because it simply made sense to you at the time, became powerful messages that you felt, heard, and saw (three) over and over again (four). Eventually these messages became beliefs, and as such, they formed the limits of your view of reality, deciding what you would or would not see and how you would evaluate each of your experiences. Outdated or inaccurate though some of them may be, you, like all of us, have most likely continued to accept at least some inaccurate beliefs because they are what you know and trust.

It's not easy to take a long-held belief, even a negative one, and hold it up to the light of serious examination. It is difficult enough that, under ordinary circumstances, you probably wouldn't even think of doing so. This is where anger comes to your rescue. Anger creates an extraordinary situation. It shakes up your belief system by forcefully presenting you with an experience that does not fit your internal image of what should and must be. Anger, by highlighting an experience that is more than you can currently handle calmly, also highlights the fact that the offending experience doesn't fit with the expectations created by your beliefs. Doing so, it invites you in stage two to take a deeper look at those beliefs.

In the following chapters, where you will explore and make use of the gift-of-anger process, you will find many examples of people updating their beliefs, healing inner pain, and successfully increasing their level of freedom and joy with the help of their anger. For now, consider an example that doesn't depend on anger. It occurred as a result of a research project, and I include it here because it so clearly demonstrates what can happen when you put into use the four rules that create and integrate a belief.

The Langer Study

In 1979, Dr. Ellen J. Langer, a professor of psychology at Harvard University, conducted a study of a group of men who were between seventy-five and eighty years old and in reasonably good health. She divided the men into two groups, control and experimental. As she explained in her book *Mindfulness* (1989), part of this study involved taking the experimental group to a secluded country retreat. Langer asked them not to bring along any photographs or reading materials more recent than 1959 (originating no later than twenty years earlier, when the men were in their mid-fifties). The subjects were given several tests, including tests for vision, mental speed and accuracy, and physical strength. Their height was measured and they were photographed.

The research team then asked the men to speak as if they were living twenty years earlier. They were to speak in the present tense about life as it was twenty years ago, and the team even suggested that they feel as they felt twenty years ago. In short, they were not told to act as if it were twenty years earlier. Instead, they were told to *be* who they were twenty years earlier (the ultimate acting job!). The interior decor, the reading material, any discussions the men had, the food they ate, the television shows they saw, and the movies they watched all conformed to what would have been normal twenty years earlier.

These seventy-five- to eighty-year-old men imagined themselves twenty years younger (*rule one is to present something as actual fact*). They followed instructions by acting as if they absolutely believed what they imagined (*rule two is to act like you truly believe it*). They used all of their senses, in that everything they saw, heard, tasted, smelled, or discussed was as it would have been twenty years earlier (*rule three is to make your statements emotionally powerful, using as many of the five senses as possible*). They lived together in this location and under these circumstances for five days (*rule four is to repeat over time*). At the end of the fourth day, they were retested and rephotographed.

Now stop for a moment and notice your own expectations here. What do you think the new tests showed? Do you believe that when the men were tested four days later the results revealed them to be four days older? A year older? Younger? How much younger? What are your expectations? Okay, now here are the results.

The evaluations of independent judges attested that the men looked about three years younger. Testing showed that their hearing had improved, as had their memories. Their hand grips were stronger. They were acting more independently, including taking better care of themselves rather than waiting for others to care for them. They showed increased manual dexterity, and their sitting height had actually increased (presumably from sitting up straighter).

All of these changes happened in a mere four days! Dr. Langer and her research team had changed the expectations of the men who participated in her study, and the men's changed expectations had led to new feelings and behavior that more accurately reflected their true capacity.

No matter what your beliefs, you cannot behave in ways that are physically impossible. Had these men been living to their capacity in the first place, there would have been no change in their behavior. In fact, what this experiment seems to suggest is both how greatly their beliefs about age and about themselves affected their feelings and behavior and how limiting their beliefs had been. Dr. Langer changed their frame of reference, and in doing so, unlocked some of their previously unknown potential.

The Power of Frame of Reference

Your *frame of reference* is your personal view of yourself and the world, formed and held securely in place by your beliefs. If you think of your beliefs as forming an actual frame through which you view yourself and the rest of life, you can get an idea of how solid and potentially rigid your frame of reference is. Imagine it as a picture frame, formed by those beliefs that you accept as dependably accurate and incorporating all of your expectations that result from your beliefs. Like a picture frame, your frame of reference focuses your attention on what's inside the frame—on the particular, limited interpretation of yourself and what is happening in your life that your accepted beliefs guide you to make. As a result, you're usually not aware of the truths about yourself or your world that are outside your frame of reference. You may not even be aware that there *is* an "outside."

We all make sense of our experiences by interpreting them according to our individual frames of reference, solidly formed by our personal beliefs. With our frames of reference steadfastly in place, we interpret our own actions and those of others in a way that is reliable to us and perhaps even comforting in its predictability. Operating repeatedly within the limits of our individual frames, we do not realize how much of life we may be missing. The men in Dr. Langer's study, for instance, probably had no idea of their unused potential until their frames of reference were modified by their intense focus on being twenty years younger. Imagine their surprise when their looks and behavior improved as a result.

You probably don't have a research project, but you do have your anger. Your anger can highlight an opportunity for you to move beyond a limiting belief. Then, as you do so, you will expand your frame of reference so that you see yourself and the world more accurately and fully, making some of your own unused potential available to you as a result. Let's review how this can happen. While you will learn more information as you practice the seven steps in the upcoming chapters, let's put together what you've learned so far about how anger can further your awareness and your growth beyond your previously held limitations.

Putting It All Together

Anger often starts with a belief about yourself or about others that is inaccurate and constricting, held firmly, and sometimes held out of sight. The constriction causes upsetting and painful feelings. When you are caught in a present-day experience that awakens your pain, you define the experience as unfair, hurtful, or in some other way wrong. Because your constricting belief is involved and because you are in pain as a result, you feel unable to calmly and easily right the wrong or tolerate the situation as it is. Taken together, these three factors—defining the situation as unfair or wrong, feeling unable to change it, and feeling unable to tolerate it as it is—trigger your anger, which emerges to protect you by adding to your strength and loosening your inhibitions. You are now in stage one.

As soon as the immediate experience has passed, perhaps as briefly as a few seconds or perhaps much longer, you have the option to either remain in stage one and very likely have other similarly upsetting experiences in the future, or to move to stage two. Stage two is a quieter stage, and one that you can enter only by choice.

In stage two, you can use the gift-of-anger process to help you heal your pain and update your inaccurate and constricting belief. Doing so over time weakens your old belief and installs your new, more accurate understanding. Your frame of reference widens as a result, and you can see yourself and those around you more fully and clearly. The energy that used to be held in the form of constriction is released, and you may feel a sense of expansion and well-being. You have become more than you were because you have gained both the wisdom and the increased potential to enjoy your life that a wider frame of reference brings. As a result, you see reality more accurately and can live more joyfully.

It can be a continuing, positive spiral. With your frame of reference widened and an old wound healed, you become freer and more expansive. You become better able to care for yourself while viewing both yourself and those around you with more understanding and compassion. You have made good use of your anger in stage two. Now you can relax and enjoy the results—until life brings another experience made difficult because it collides with a belief in need of updating. Then the process begins anew.

It is an elegant system when understood and used consciously. The blocks to your full awareness cause your anger, which then highlights your current block and both fuels and guides your release from it. Then, sooner or later, your anger highlights another block. It can be a continuous system, one that can repeatedly increase your awareness and your growth.

Like anyone else, you have an ongoing choice to widen your frame of reference or not. The capacity to do so is built into everyone. You have the potential for seeing yourself, the people around you, and your world ever more fully and clearly. You have the potential to become increasingly more in charge of your responses to life, increasingly better able to hold and resolve the difficulties that come your way. Your anger is a key that can unlock this potential. It will continue to remind you that it is always available to help you grow beyond your current experience. It will continue to clamor for your attention, asking and sometimes demanding that you take this next important and healing step.

Beginning the Process

Now that you have explored the stages, attributes, and purpose of your anger, seeing how it works to help you become more conscious and more capable in your life, you're ready to use the gift-of-anger process. In the remaining chapters, we'll be focusing on each of the seven steps of this process in order. There are explanations of each step, guidelines on how to use and personalize the process, and examples of others who have worked with it and grown from it. You will also find a separate chapter, chapter 11, in which you will learn specific directions for using this process when you are angry with yourself.

The hope is not for you to simply learn the process, but for you to personalize it and make it your own. In that way it will become natural to you. It will become a tool that remains available to you, helping you to deepen your knowledge and friendship with yourself while increasing your understanding and successful navigation of the world around you.

CHAPTER 4

Step One: Acknowledge Your Anger and Safely Regain Your Emotional Balance

The first step in the gift-of-anger process is a transitional one, designed to bring you from stage one into stage two. To begin this step, you will need a way to recognize that you are, in fact, angry. Then, you can complete step one by using a stress-management technique to help you regain your emotional balance. Doing so will enable you to focus your attention on the healing and empowering information you will discover as you explore your anger using the rest of the process.

Discovering Your Personal Cue

You begin step one by identifying your *personal anger cue,* a signal you can rely on to alert you to the fact that you're angry and can now begin to complete the seven steps. Identifying and using your cue can help you in a couple of ways. The first and most obvious benefit is that by identifying and learning to recognize your personal anger cue, you become aware of when you're angry. This is an important step for those who may not realize that they are angry until well into the angering experience or even after it has occurred. You may be in this group, especially if you have been taught either to avoid anger or to fall quickly and impulsively into it.

The second benefit to identifying and using your personal anger cue is that it will help you to take charge of anger ever more quickly, easily, and dependably. You will begin to notice your cue sooner and with more assurance and use it as a signal to complete step one. This is a key to using your anger rather than becoming stuck in it—the beginning of your having anger rather than your anger having and controlling you. This is how you start using your anger in stage two.

While you may have times when acting on your anger seems most important, knowing that you can use your cue as a signal to use the process will change your definition of anger. Quickly noticing your cue will remind you that you have the *choice* to move to stage two and focus the power of your anger. When you do so, your anger serves to help you to clear your vision, better understand both yourself and what is truly going on, and determine your best response. Anger will have become a sign of your potential for increasing your awareness and enhancing your personal growth rather than just a signal of impending confrontation.

A Variety of Cues

There are so many potential anger cues that listing them all would be impossible. But you can use the following examples as a starting point to help you observe yourself and identify your own most reliable sign. The guideline to use in identifying your cue is that it should be one that occurs each time you are angry and is noticeable enough to get your attention.

Physical cues. Clients and workshop participants have identified several physical cues, including rapid breathing, faster heartbeat, clenched jaw, sweaty palms, tight chest, headache, tensed muscles, and upset stomach. Notice that these can also be signs of illness. Anger in stage one, like illness, erases your sense of well-being such that, if you react as many people do, you may actually feel ill when you become angry. If so, using your personal anger cue may improve your sense of well-being even when you're actively angry, because using this signal reminds you that you have a choice in how you interpret the purpose of your anger. You have the choice to move to stage two.

Mental cues. When angry, people often think in terms that are absolute. Someone is definitely wrong. A situation is absolutely unfair. Something just shouldn't be! The extenuating circumstances of the situation or the positive attributes of the other person are crowded out of awareness by the impact of anger, and all that you can see is *the problem*. This narrowing of focus to a pinpoint awareness of the problem alone is often an indicator of anger. Even very loving couples can forget that they love each other in the heat of anger. Friends can forget their closeness as all of their attention concentrates on the other person's misbehavior and how unfair or "wrong" it is. Blame is one form of narrowed focus, one many of my clients have chosen as their personal anger cue.

Emotional cues. Some people report that they feel numb when angry because their anger frightens them or they have been taught that it's unacceptable. When angry, they may say pleasantly appropriate words and yet feel disconnected from their emotions and their body until safely away from the experience and the danger they ascribe to it. Then their anger emerges as their true thoughts and feelings become clear.

At the other end of the emotional scale, anger can cause agitation and tears. People may cry because they are overwhelmed by their feelings. They are unable to marshal their thoughts and effectively take charge because they are lost in a wave of angry emotion. They may also cry if they have been taught that anger is not okay but tears are acceptable.

Perhaps the most noticeable emotional cue, however, is the one felt not as a presence but as an absence: the absence of the ability to stay calm and solve the problem at hand. *Adrenaline*, a hormone released in your body when you're angry, keeps you feeling irritated and unable to think calmly and clearly.

Determining Your Own Cue

The personal anger cues we've just reviewed provide you with a starting place from which you can begin to determine your own anger cues. Observing your experiences over time, you can notice which cue most obviously and reliably works for you. Then, as you establish the pattern of noticing this cue, you can more quickly and easily identify the fact that you're mad and begin the process. That's what Janet, Hal, and Kristin did in the stories that follow.

Janet

Janet, who first used the gift-of-anger process when she was angry with her family doctor for misdiagnosing her symptoms and dismissing her pain, noticed three main, reliable cues to the presence of her anger. The first was jaw tension. Janet said that she would feel discomfort in her jaw and, focusing on it to see what was wrong, she would notice that she had rigidly tensed her jaw muscles. Janet's second clue was her speech. She found that when she became angry, the pace of her words would quicken and the tone of her voice would rise. Her final cue was that her focus would turn to blame. Her statements, whether spoken internally to herself or out loud to others, became unequivocal. The offending person was "wrong" and "bad." Whatever had happened was all their fault. It was this last cue, the desire to emphatically blame the other person, which was the strongest and most obvious for Janet. She came to trust this cue to reliably and quickly identify her own angering experiences and begin the process.

⑾ Hal

Hal, a workshop attendee, noticed that just thinking about his brother resulted in discomfort as his face flushed and his jaw tightened. At the same time, he could feel his hands ball into fists. "The cues seem to happen together," he said. "I really notice them all." What he also noticed was the extent of his anger. Hal had a history of unexamined angry encounters with his brother, a history that took many repetitions of the process to learn deeply from and move beyond. Thinking about his anger cues, Hal decided to track them and see if they emerged reliably. Doing so, he found that he could count most on his jaw tightening each time to signal that he was becoming angry and cue him to begin the gift-of-anger process.

⑾ Kristin

Kristin, furious with a coworker who always found a reason for taking extra breaks and refused to do her share of the work, noticed over time that her chief cue was feeling sick to her stomach. Kristin had been taught not to focus on anger at all. Instead, she had learned to stuff her feelings down, usually by eating. As Kristin lessened her reliance on food and paid more attention to what her stomach was really telling her, she found that she had to move slowly through this process. At first, not being used to feeling her anger directly, she found its power scary. With time and practice, however, Kristin learned to trust herself and to handle the intensity of her emotions with increasing assurance. That increase in inner strength and self-trust filled her as no food ever had.

Once Janet, Hal, and Kristin identified and began to watch for their clearest anger cue, they began to notice the presence of their anger more quickly and, eventually, at more benign levels. You can do the same thing, and doing so sets you firmly on the path of your stage-two process.

EXERCISE: Identifying Your Personal Anger Cue

Now that you've seen how important it is to identify your personal anger signals, you can use this exercise to begin doing so:

1. To identify your anger cue, pick a memory of a mild-to-moderate experience of anger and review it in your mind to determine how you knew you were mad. Often, simply remembering an angry experience will bring up some of the upset feelings that were originally attached to it. If this is true for you, notice where and how you experience those feelings now. You can also review the cues introduced earlier to help you identify which ones are most familiar to you.

2. Identify the cue or couple of cues that either stand out in your memory of this experience or seem most familiar when reading the list. Write them down in your anger journal.

3. Now that you have recorded your potential anger cues, redo this exercise using two or three memories of other angering experiences of varying intensities. Notice which of your identified cues repeatedly captures your attention the most. Remember that Janet repeatedly noticed blaming, Hal noticed his jaw tightening, and Kristin reliably noticed her stomach feeling upset. What cue comes up for you? Again, write it down.

4. Look for the emergence of your identified anger cue as you go through your week. If you are satisfied that it reliably signals that your anger is present, then you have your personal anger cue. If you don't find this cue reliable, repeat the exercise so that you can identify the cue that will most dependably and intensely alert you to your own anger.

5. Once you have identified your personal anger cue, you can be on the lookout for it. As noticing it becomes a habit, you may find yourself more quickly becoming aware of your anger. Doing so, you may notice that many of your angry experiences become less intense because you catch them faster and then have the expecta-

tion of using them productively by completing the rest of the steps in the process.

Scanning for Anger

If you have difficulty identifying a dependable anger cue, you might try doing a *body scan.* Scanning in this way is a particular way of focusing on your internal experience of your body and then checking your mental and emotional states. You can quickly do a body scan periodically throughout your day, as well as whenever you believe you might be angry. Doing so will help you to identify your personal anger cue as the scan trains you to more fully notice what is happening internally, perhaps just beyond your normal awareness. As you become proficient in using this technique, you'll be able to use it anytime, either standing or sitting, and with your eyes open. For the first few times, though, it can help your concentration to sit down and close your eyes.

How to Do a Body Scan

To perform a body scan, slowly move your focus internally from your feet, up your legs, up through the trunk of your body, shoulders, arms and hands, neck, and head. As you pay attention to each of these different parts of your body, look for any muscle tightness, aches, pain, or numbness that you might feel. These uncomfortable sensations could, of course, signal a physical problem, and you should certainly seek medical attention any time you feel the need. However, these sensations can also signal anger, so if you become aware of discomfort as you move your awareness up through your body, pay attention to your thoughts and feelings to determine whether or not you are also angry. If you are, notice the cues your body, mind, and emotions are giving you, and especially notice which cue is the strongest.

If you've never previously done a body scan, the procedure may seem awkward and time consuming at first. Keep doing it, however, and you will soon notice that the process becomes easier, faster, and more automatic. Once you are used to it, a body scan can be done in less than a minute.

EXERCISE: Performing a Body Scan

Sitting down and with eyes closed, slowly bring your awareness up through your body, paying special attention to any tightness or discomfort in your stomach, chest, shoulders, or jaw. These are areas where many clients have reported holding the tension that comes with anger. As you internally check each part of your body, answer the following:

- Are your thoughts peaceful or agitated?
- What are you feeling? Are you relaxed or upset? If upset, in what way are you upset, and what do you believe caused this feeling?
- How is your breathing? Is it calm? Rapid? Clear and easy? Or is it constricted or difficult in some way?

Doing this exercise a few times each day can make it much easier to recognize when you're feeling anger and can help you to identify a reliable anger cue. To aid yourself further, write your findings in your anger journal at least the first few times you perform your body scan. You will then have a written account of the signals your body, mind, and emotions are giving you throughout your day and can begin to see patterns that tell you when you're angry and which cue most strongly signals that anger. Eventually, you will most likely find yourself noticing your cue almost immediately. It will have become second nature to you to be aware of it and to use it to help you regain your sense of balance.

Once you have identified your most obvious and reliable anger cue, you won't need to repeat this initial part of step one. Recognizing your chosen anger cue as it comes up, you can go immediately to the second part of this step.

Regaining Your Emotional Balance

Once you become proficient at recognizing your anger cue, you may find that you sometimes notice your anger at such benign levels that you do not need to calm down and regain your emotional balance in order to think clearly. Almost everyone, however, has times when the seriousness of the upsetting event necessitates finding a way to calm the irritated feelings that anger can bring. You can't be expected to think deeply or creatively while experiencing the irritable rush of energy that can accompany anger. Reducing your stress level needs to come first.

Using a stress-management technique to regain your sense of balance is the second part of step one. The goal here is to calm yourself without risking unnecessary escalation of the problem.

You may already know and use the techniques that follow, or you may have other stress-management techniques that work very well for you. If so, you can quickly review this section and then move to the next chapter. If any of these techniques are new to you, however, you may want to add them to your repertoire. Since life is so often unpredictable and angering experiences can happen when you least expect them, you will find methods here that can be used in a variety of settings and within various time limits. As you read the descriptions of each method, pick out those that you would feel most comfortable using.

Breathe diaphragmatically. One of the easiest methods to discharge adrenaline and reduce emotional stress is to use deep breathing, often called *diaphragmatic breathing*. This is something that you can do anywhere and, even if your anger is too great for your adrenaline to be completely discharged with this method, it's a good way to initiate the discharge process.

If you're new to diaphragmatic breathing, it would probably be easiest to start lying down. In this position, you'll be better able to discern your belly rising and falling with breath. Lie down and put one hand on your belly and one on your chest. Comfortably inhale all the way down into your belly, noticing your hand rise as your belly expands while the hand on your chest stays relatively still. Then exhale slowly, noting that the hand on your belly naturally descends. I call this "sloppy breathing" because you let your stomach stick out as you breathe in and your diaphragm fills with air. Then your stomach naturally flattens as you breathe out. Breathing this way helps you release your diaphragm, chest, and stomach muscles, which often contract when one becomes angry. By releasing those contracted muscles, you automatically help your body to relax.

Take an exercise break. Any safe physical exercise is another method to consider, one that makes good use of your adrenaline-fueled energy and leaves you feeling calmer and thinking with a clearer perspective. If you have the time and are able, take a walk. This is a healthy way to create enough mental and emotional space to do some calmer, clearer thinking.

Talk it out. You can talk to a friend or someone else you trust, keeping in mind that getting answers from your friend is not the goal. Instead, the objective is for you to describe the situation and how you feel about it so that you can calm yourself in the process. Talking through what happened often reduces tension. As well, it may enable you to recall details that you might have forgotten.

If you use this technique, make sure that the friend you speak with is levelheaded and detached enough to listen to you and help you regain your sense of balance. What you don't want is someone who will become angry in support of you and join you in your adrenaline rush.

Write a poison-pen letter. Another method, one that I teach when I give workshops, is to write a poison-pen letter. I use this particular method for discharging anger because it can be done in a variety of places, from work settings, to home, to sitting in your car or even out on a park bench.

A *poison-pen letter* is a very special letter that you write to the person with whom you're angry, telling that person everything that upset you about your experience with him or her and sharing, frankly and completely, all of your negative feelings about the person and about the event. You write the letter, but you do *not* send it. Instead, you say everything that you are filled with, all the accusations, all the name-calling, all the self-defending, all the reasons why you're right and the other person is wrong. Then, with your adrenaline safely encased in the pages of your letter, you destroy the letter, knowing that you are now ready to explore your thoughts and feelings more calmly, deeply, and fully. This is the one exercise that does not belong in your anger journal. Write it out on separate sheets of paper so that you can destroy it after you're done.

You are writing out whatever is fueling your anger, so if you choose this method, give yourself the time to be thorough so that you rid yourself of as much of your irritation as possible. This is not a time to worry about grammar, punctuation, or spelling. In fact, you might find that your feelings spill out onto the page so quickly that your writing is illegible. That's okay. You're not going to keep this letter. The point is simply to get your adrenaline-fueled feelings out in a safe and thorough way. This process may take a few minutes, or it may take an hour. Give yourself permission to write whatever is inside you, without censoring it, until you feel done.

Many people have been shocked and embarrassed by what they write, alarmed at the vitriol of their words. The fact is that the poison of these words has been inside you. How healthy to free yourself from that poison and to know that the anger that may have seemed endless and overwhelming is now contained within the finite limits of the paper. Even more healthful is the realization that by emptying out your adrenaline-laced anger, you have created a safe space within you where you can now more thoughtfully focus on your exploration and healing process.

As a final act of writing your poison-pen letter, after you feel completely finished, congratulate yourself for being open to this process, thorough in your writing, and true to your feelings. Then, as an affirmation that you are ready to move beyond the limits of your initial anger, destroy your poison-pen letter in any way that feels right.

These are a few of the methods that you can use to regain your perspective, and you might think of others that work even better for you. The goal is to safely discharge your adrenaline without harming yourself or anyone else.

⑾ Kristin

Kristin, angry with her coworker for taking extra breaks and refusing to do her share of the work, preferred to take a brisk walk to defuse her anger. However, this was often impossible to do when she was working. So when at work, she wrote a poison-pen letter instead.

In her description of this step, Kristin said that her words almost gushed out onto the paper, her writing almost illegible in her rush to get her feelings out. As soon as she gave herself permission to write whatever she felt, regardless of content, grammar, or penmanship, the words simply flew out of her pen. Usually a calm, caring person, Kristin's language became caustic and attacking. Out came her fury at her colleague for doing so little. Out came swearing. Out came name-calling. Out came accusations of being a worthless team member and being lazy and self-centered. Kristin wrote until her initial rush of emotion was spent. She knew that she was done when the words stopped coming and she felt calmer. She then safely tucked the letter away, to be burned in her fireplace at home as a further act of releasing her anger.

⑾ Kirk

Diligent, knowledgeable, and likable, Kirk had worked his way up to the position of assistant manager in a local hardware store. He had been in this position for about six months when a friend of the manager started working there, too. Soon after, the manager told Kirk that he had been receiving complaints about Kirk and fired him. Kirk was sure that there had been no complaints and suspected that the manager would fill the now-open position with his friend.

Kirk took an exercise break to release his charged feelings. An accomplished tennis player, he began the gift-of-anger process by smashing tennis balls against a backboard. He hit the ball over and over again until, at last, he exhaled in an audible sigh, realizing that he was tired and much calmer. He was then ready for step two.

⑾ Jennifer

Jennifer is an acquaintance of mine who read the prepublication manuscript of this book as a favor to me, all the while believing that she never became angry. Reading this chapter changed her mind.

Out of curiosity, Jennifer decided to regularly practice doing a body scan. As a result, she noticed how often she felt mildly annoyed, just a bit frustrated. It was nothing she could not easily manage, and, in fact, she had long ago gotten used to the feelings. However, periodic body scans showed her just how prevalent her frustration was and that it tended to settle in her tightened stomach and chest.

Curious about how diaphragmatic breathing would affect the muscles in these areas, Jennifer began taking three slow, diaphragmatic breaths a few times during her day. Each time she did so, she pretended she was breathing right into the tight muscles, loosening them and giving them ease and space.

It was after a few days of this practice that she had a hunch that her constant, low-level annoyance was caused by her continually trying to get "one more thing" done. Passionate about her work, often trying to fit more into a day than was possible, she wondered if her low-level anger indicated a need to take more time for herself. To find out, Jennifer continued to perform her body scan, increasing the frequency so that she performed a body scan every hour. Each time she did so, she focused three diaphragmatic breaths on each place of tightness or discomfort. She was surprised by how much better she felt when she did this. Calmer and feeling periodically recharged during her day, Jennifer still got almost as much done and began to enjoy her work and her life much more fully.

EXERCISE: Make an Agreement with Yourself

You have now reviewed some methods for regaining your sense of calm and balance after you've become angry. Maybe you've even thought of your own methods as well. Your next step is to complete the following:

1. Choose the one or two methods you would feel most comfortable using.

2. Write them down in your journal, along with your personal anger cue. Doing so will remind you that you are making an agreement with yourself to use your personal anger cue and then to follow with one of the calming techniques you have chosen.

3. Begin immediately to use your cue and your chosen calming technique. Then, notice as they become habitual aids to working with your anger positively.

If you realize that you've become angry and forgotten to use these tools, don't waste time becoming upset with yourself. Simply use your cue and the stress-management technique that best fits your situation as soon as you realize the need. As you do so, you'll find yourself remembering sooner and acting more quickly. You are establishing a new and healthy pattern, one that moves you gently and firmly into stage two.

Choose Your Experience

You will need to use an experience that still angers you somewhat in order to complete the rest of the steps in the seven-step process. The best experience to use is a small-to-medium one, an experience that upsets you but does not evoke your fury. Why? Imagine going to a gym to learn how to lift weights. You wouldn't start by lifting two hundred pounds, would you? That would be too much weight for someone who hadn't yet practiced using the equipment or developed the muscles to lift that much weight. Instead, you would start fairly small, becoming better able to handle more weight with each trip to the gym. In the same way, don't start with a two-hundred-pound anger experience. Be kind to yourself by learning the entire process first and practicing it a few times.

EXERCISE:
Complete Step One of the Gift-of-Anger Process

Once you've chosen the experience you want to work with, complete the following:

1. With the experience and the anger it evoked firmly in mind, notice the presence of your personal anger cue.

2. If the memory of your experience is still upsetting enough, pick one of your rebalancing techniques and use it with this experience.

3. Write the results in your journal.

Now that you have a record of your completion of step one, it's almost time to discuss the second step. First, though, let's do a brief review.

The Gift-of-Anger Process

As chapter 4 draws to a close, let's take a quick look back at each element of step one of the gift-of-anger process. Remember, you can always return to this list (or any previous chapter) if you need a reminder or some encouragement. The steps are:

1. **Recognize Your Anger...**

Learn your:

- Physical symptoms

- Mental patterns

- Associated feelings

so that you can identify your most reliable personal anger cue.

And Regain Your Emotional Balance

Take private time to:

- Breathe diaphragmatically

- Take an exercise break

- Talk it out

- Write a poison-pen letter

- Or use any other method that safely releases your adrenaline without causing harm, either to yourself or to anyone else

Now you're ready for step two.

CHAPTER 5

Step Two: Notice Your Thoughts and Feelings

Once you've become aware of your anger and used a safe method to discharge your initial rush of emotion, you are ready to begin working more closely with the actual angering experience. As you may remember, a situation will evoke your anger when it awakens tender, painful feelings that cause you to define the situation as 1) unfair or wrong, 2) difficult to change, and 3) more than you can tolerate. These are the three factors that, taken together, trigger anger. Your goal now, in this second step of the process, is to explore the presence of these three factors in the particular situation that you're working with and to identify the painful feelings that initiated their presence.

Explore Your Memory of Your Experience

Begin your investigation by thoroughly describing to yourself what happened in the anger-provoking experience, carefully reviewing what was said or done to you, what you thought and felt, and how you responded. It helps to pay special attention to your thoughts and feelings about what occurred both during and after the episode. Do this in as much detail as you can recall.

This is a time to explain to yourself the specific way or ways your angering experience seemed unfair to you. Doing so will help you increase your understanding of what made it difficult or impossible for you to change the upsetting situation and add to your knowledge of what it was about this specific experience that made it more than you could tolerate without the added power boost of your anger. Your thoughts and feelings during and after the experience can give you this information. Your memory of what occurred contains a gold mine of information about you and about your view of the world, information that will help you to more fully comprehend yourself, your painful experience, and your anger. As with any mine, you have to know where to dig. In this case, dig into your memory for your thoughts and feelings.

What you're doing may sound like another poison-pen letter, but in fact, it's quite different. With a poison-pen letter, you are writing to the person with whom you are angry. Your goal is to discharge your adrenaline by giving that person (in your imagination) the full extent of your wrath. Now, in step two, you are focusing on gaining a better, more complete understanding of yourself and your world. All of us need to be heard and understood, but too often we don't take the time to really hear and understand ourselves. This is your opportunity to explain yourself to your most important audience—you.

You will benefit most from this step by writing down your experience and your thoughts and feelings about it in your anger journal. You already know that writing down your answers to the exercises in this book will give you a permanent record of your discoveries about anger and about your progress in working with it. You will also be using the answers you uncover in this step to help you complete the two steps that follow. There are other reasons to write down your answers, though, reasons that make it well worth your time and effort to do so.

Writing Contains Your Anger

Anger can seem like too much to handle, even after the immediate adrenaline rush has passed. If you can contain your experience on a sheet of paper or even ten sheets, then it usually feels more manageable. One of the reasons this happens is that writing it all down helps stop the mental process that keeps you repeatedly recalling the same details. That circular pattern of retracing the event over and over in your mind can exhaust you without accomplishing anything useful. Instead, when you can see your experience on paper, you can also see it clearly delineated into a beginning, middle, and end. You can then access each phase easily, rather than needing to mentally recall it yet again.

Writing Enhances Your Memory as It Slows Your Mind

As you write, you may find yourself remembering details that you had forgotten, details that may be important. You may also remember other, similar experiences that help make this one more understandable. You may think of applicable wisdom that you hadn't ever considered before.

This enhancement of your memory and of your ability to make mental connections between what happened in your current situation and in other, similar situations occurs, in part, because writing slows you down. Rather than thinking through the experience quickly and automatically, as we all have learned to do, writing takes more time. This added time presents opportunities for more awareness to arise.

Moving more slowly and thoughtfully, you create the potential for your mind to make new connections, to see things in a way that doesn't necessarily agree with your normal, well-established presumptions. Instead, you can allow yourself to act like a detective, following the clues to see where they lead.

How to Write a Self-Discovery Letter

You can complete step two by writing a *self-discovery letter*. This is a letter to yourself in which you deeply and fully explore what happened that upset you, including the thoughts and feelings you had during and after your angering experience. Many people have found that writing a letter to themselves felt more intimate than simply writing down information, and it enabled them to be more thoughtful and forthcoming with themselves as well.

Create a Comfortable, Private Space

You can begin by creating a comfortable, private space, one where you know that you can write whatever you wish and take as much time as you need. It's a good idea to turn your phone off so you won't be interrupted. Have your anger journal with you and extra pens as well. You can write the letter using a computer and then keep your completed letter with your journal, but many people have said that the experience feels more meaningful when done with paper and pen. You might experiment and see which medium works best for you.

Be a Good Friend to Yourself

When you have created a comfortable space, get comfortable inside as well. You can do so by taking a few deep breaths to soften your belly muscles and then imagining opening your heart. Then, begin your letter by writing, "Dear (your name)."

Your goal is to understand yourself and your experience more fully and to be a caring ally to yourself in the process. As you write your letter, imagine that you are pouring your heart out to your very best friend, one with whom you can share all of your thoughts and feelings, all of the details of your upsetting experience. Take yourself as seriously as you wish the offending person would. Being an attentive, understanding friend to yourself will help you more than anyone else's attention ever could.

Several people have said that their grammar, punctuation, and spelling all suffered during the writing of this letter. That's fine. This is your letter, just for you. Don't worry about grammar, punctuation, or spelling as you write it. Just let your thoughts and feelings write themselves out onto the page.

At this point, you've already released much of your adrenaline by completing the first step; however, you might still have a fair amount of emotion left. If so, this is the place to let it out. One client said that name-calling, self-pity, feeling small, and crying all played a part in her completion of this step. On the other hand, you may find that you are ready to focus solely on a thoughtful examination of what happened and what it means to you. Either way is fine. Simply pay attention to your own needs and do this step as fully and completely as you can.

Explore Your Experience Completely

Recount your experience during and after the event, including your thoughts and your feelings, and explain how the three factors that trigger anger were present in your experience. Include any feelings that arise in you as you write and any further information that comes to you. You can use the following questions as guidelines if you wish:

- ⫶ What happened?

- ⫶ What was the worst thing about your experience, and how did that make you feel?

- ⫶ What had you hoped for but did not get? Or, what happened that you wish hadn't?

- ⫶ How did you judge the situation? The other person? Yourself?

- ⫶ What made this situation hard to correct? To tolerate?

- ⫶ What other emotions did you feel besides anger?

- ⫶ Did your thoughts or feelings change at all during the experience? Afterward? How?

- ⫶ Are these thoughts and feelings familiar? How so?

If you find that you have trouble writing or that you don't have much to say, this may be an indication that you are not used to this kind of process. If so, I suggest that you stay with the exercise for at least another ten minutes. You may end up taking a lot more time, and that's fine. But stay with it for at least ten more minutes. Doing so will give you time to get used to writing and afford an opportunity to go beneath the surface, to do more than just a superficial inquiry.

Notice any minimizing. As you write, pay attention to any inclination you may have to explain away what happened or make immediate allowances for the other person.

So many people have been taught to make light of their anger and pain and to focus only on the positive. One client noticed this tendency when she found herself writing, "Oh, this is so awful. I'm looking at the negative. I shouldn't focus on the negative. I should see the other side. I should look for the positives."

The problem with thinking this way is that it doesn't work. It may, in fact, make you angrier, because what you're telling yourself is that you don't have a right to your feelings. This is neither helpful nor true. Remember that the goal of this letter is to write out your thoughts and feelings fully and honestly. That means letting your exploration take you where it will and writing it all out. When you do, and when you continue following the rest of the process, your feelings will most likely change by themselves. What you are doing now is simply one step in a seven-step process, so trust yourself.

Don't stop until you're sure you're finished. Write until you feel finished, and then ask yourself if there's more. You might check your belly. Does it feel relaxed and easy, or does it feel tight or upset (perhaps indicating that you have more to write)? Then check your heart and again ask if you're finished or if you have more writing to do. You owe it to yourself to be thorough.

Congratulate yourself. When you feel totally finished with your letter, congratulate yourself for being open to this self-exploration process and thorough in your writing. Your self-discovery letter will form the foundation for completing your next two steps and, when added to future self-discovery letters, may help you clarify and perhaps heal a long-time anger pattern.

⑾ Valerie

Valerie was a member of the program committee of her church and was upset because she felt that her ideas had been ignored at a particular meeting. Having discharged her adrenaline by writing a poison-pen letter, Valerie found herself writing more thoughtfully in her self-discovery letter. She noticed that she explored what happened in greater detail and examined her thoughts and feelings more thoroughly. Giving herself the time and space to write comfortably and without interruption, she filled five pages before finishing this exercise.

As part of her self-discovery letter, Valerie wrote, "I hate being on this committee. I give so much of my time, and then I'm ignored. I feel minimized and dictated to. I'm invisible to them except to do whatever they decide I should do *for them*. My ideas don't count. They don't even listen to me. They're just so full of themselves. And I go along with them—why do I do that? Why don't I stand up for myself? Why don't I just leave?"

Having written these questions, Valerie soon ended her self-discovery letter. She had hit upon some very important questions and didn't yet have any answers to them. It was time to move to the next steps so that she could uncover her answers and make use of them.

⑾ Denise

Denise had been trying to help a friend whose insurance company had denied his claim. While her friend felt the denial made sense and was ready to accept the disappointing situation and move on, Denise insisted that the ruling was unfair and angrily vowed to write a letter on his behalf. Encouraged to explore her anger by writing a self-discovery letter, she began to cry as she wrote, "I shouldn't have to do this. I'm too young."

Denise had used the seven-step process many times before, and she immediately thought about how she had developed strong feelings about right and wrong while growing up. As a child, she had had the role of protecting her younger, weaker siblings, even though she was young herself. Now her siblings were grown and able to take care of themselves, but Denise had simply maintained her old role and transferred her "protection" to others whom she saw as weak and needy. As she picked up her pen to begin writing, her long-hidden feelings about being too young to carry the burden of protecting others emerged.

Your unconscious contains so much more information than your conscious mind can hold. When you open to a process of self-inquiry such as this one, your unconscious mind can give you information that illuminates the outdated or incorrect belief that might be fueling your anger. This is what happened to Denise. Growing up, she hadn't been able to access her feelings of overwhelm at having to protect and parent her siblings at such a young age. Now it was safe to examine them. So out they came, giving Denise a chance to set herself free from an unnecessarily constricting pattern by exploring and updating her old feelings and the belief that produced them.

"I've always tried to make things 'right,'" she said, "always saw it as my responsibility. I guess it's time to let that go. I just don't want to be everyone's protector anymore."

Eric

Eric moved to New Mexico from the East Coast in order to start a new job. Hoping that the move would be easy and uneventful, he instead endured a nightmare of lost and broken possessions and moving-company personnel who seemed focused only on avoiding responsibility.

At first, Eric was so angry at the amount of destruction and the callous attitude of the claims adjuster that all he could do was think murderous thoughts while muttering furiously to himself about their incompetence. Diaphragmatic breathing began to calm him down, but he had to take a five-mile run before feeling that he could sit down and write a self-discovery letter. Doing so, he wrote about how admiring of his furniture and his artwork the moving-company sales representative had been and how he had assured Eric that everything would be taken care of "as if it were our own."

"Those frauds!" Eric wrote in his self-discovery letter. "How could they do this to me? They came on like my best friends. Now they've wrecked my stuff and those bastards won't even admit how incompetent they are."

Writing further, Eric surprised himself by uncovering feelings of embarrassment and self-blame that he had "let" this happen. He then wrote about feeling that he had been incompetent too. "I should have known this would happen," he wrote, "and I should have taken the time to check other companies and make sure I was getting a good mover. This is really my fault."

How many times have you, like Eric, blamed yourself when someone took advantage of you or caused you harm? It's a painful yet common pattern that a great many of us learned as children trying to make sense of a world that's way beyond a child's capacity to comprehend. Often the only conclusion that makes sense to the child is that whatever happened must have been his or her fault. Happily, this is a pattern that, as adults, we can recognize and correct. That is what Eric began to do.

As he continued to write his self-discovery letter, Eric found himself writing that his feelings of embarrassment and incompetence were familiar. "I realized how often I end up blaming myself, no matter what anyone else has done to me," he told me later.

Eric continued to think about this pattern, gaining a better understanding of it by completing the rest of the steps in the process. Gradually, he found that he could look at his situation more objectively. "Hindsight is perfect," he said. "I can always look back and think of more I could have done, but I know this wasn't my fault." Then he explained further, "The movers were worried about how this might look to their boss, so they denied responsibility. And the claims adjuster who treated me and my stuff like crap wasn't trying to ignore me or be condescending. Actually, he didn't even really *see* me. His focus was on minimizing the company's responsibility and expense as much as possible. That's the job he was hired to do." Eric ended by saying, "He needs my signature, though. He needs my agreement. So I'm not powerless like I'd feared."

As a result of his realizations, Eric was able to negotiate a settlement that worked for him. It was not perfect by any means, but it was enough, and he felt good about achieving it. He also felt good about seeing and beginning to understand his pattern of self-blame. He knew that he didn't yet understand it fully, and that he would undoubtedly have more opportunity to do so in the future. And he was ready.

A Personal Step

As you can see from these examples, step two is a very personal one. While the directions for writing a self-discovery letter are the same for everyone, you will have your own individual experience when you actually write it. Valerie wrote a five-page letter and included a series of important questions that became her focal point as she completed the rest of the steps. Denise uncovered the hidden feelings that had initiated her anger and the formerly unconscious pattern her feelings represented as well. Eric learned that even when the situation looked grim, he was not powerless. He also uncovered a pattern of self-blame that he was ready to investigate further.

Like Valerie, Denise, and Eric, you will have your own, personal experience. Simply remember to be as thorough as you can and to let whatever is inside of you come out onto the page. You may be surprised at some of the details and some of the thoughts or feelings that you find yourself writing down. On the other hand, you may give yourself information that you already had, simply validating what you already knew. You may fill a number of pages or only part of one. As long as you have taken the exercise seriously and followed the directions, any way is fine. Like everyone else's, your experience will be unique.

EXERCISE: Writing Your Self-Discovery Letter

Now it's time to write your own letter. To help you do so, complete the following:

1. Review the guidelines found in the section "How to Write a Self-Discovery Letter." They include creating a comfortable and private space to write, getting comfortable inside by taking a few deep breaths and imagining your heart opening, and refusing to minimize any of your thoughts or feelings.

2. Write your letter into your anger journal or type it separately and insert it afterwards. Either way, write your thoughts and feelings out onto the pages until you feel completely finished. When you are certain that you're done, congratulate yourself for doing this work.

Should you want help to identify your thoughts and feelings, you can review the list in the following exercise. While not a complete list by any means, you may find your own thoughts and feelings reflected there, and the list may help jog your memory as well.

EXERCISE: Sample Thoughts and Feelings

To help you access your own thoughts and feelings, you might look at the list below and circle the ones most familiar to you.

The following are typical of the thoughts mentioned afterward by people who have done the self-discovery letter exercise:

I deserve better.	I try so hard.
How could you do that to me?	I deserve to be taken care of.
My needs never count.	I've done so much for you.
You don't like me anymore.	You're just like my mother/father.
You don't care about me.	I'm not important to you.

You never listen to me.   That wasn't (you weren't) fair.

You were mean to me.   I did everything I could.

You broke your promise.   I can't stand this.

How could you treat me this way?   You lied to me.

The following are typical of the feelings mentioned afterward by people who have done the self-discovery letter exercise:

Abandoned	Helpless	Overwhelmed
Afraid	Humiliated	Rejected
Ashamed	Hurt	Shamed
Belittled	Ignored	Slighted
Betrayed	Impatient	Unappreciated
Blamed	Inadequate	Unfairly treated
Controlled	Invisible	Taken for granted
Criticized	Manipulated	Vulnerable
Disrespected	Overpowered	

When you have completed your self-discovery letter, keep it handy as you move to step three. You'll use your letter to help you complete this upcoming step, one that may be as surprising to you as it is important for increasing your personal growth and sense of well-being.

The Gift-of-Anger Process

As in the preceding chapter, let's take a moment, here at the end of chapter 5, to review the elements that make up each of the steps we've examined. The steps are:

1. **Recognize Your Anger...**

    Learn your:

    ◀|▶ Physical symptoms

    ◀|▶ Mental patterns

    ◀|▶ Associated feelings

    so that you can identify your most reliable personal anger cue.

    And Regain Your Emotional Balance

    Take private time to:

    ◀|▶ Breathe diaphragmatically

    ◀|▶ Take an exercise break

    ◀|▶ Talk it out

    ◀|▶ Write a poison-pen letter

    ◀|▶ Or use any other method that safely releases your adrenaline without causing harm, either to yourself or to anyone else

2. **Notice Your Thoughts and Feelings**

    ◀|▶ Describe the anger-provoking experience and your thoughts and feelings about it.

    ◀|▶ Write them out in a self-discovery letter.

Now it's time to move on to step three.

CHAPTER 6

Step Three: Give Yourself Validation

Writing your self-discovery letter will most likely have reminded you of the unfairness of the experience you endured and how you were right and the other person was wrong. With those feelings in mind, it's now time to give yourself *validation,* the affirmation that you were wronged by the other person and deserved better treatment from them. Affirming this to yourself is step three.

The Need for Validation

Whether you use the word validation, respect, esteem, or any other similar word, the meaning is pretty much the same. These terms mean that you feel a sense of value, an awareness that you, personally, matter. Feeling valued is not just something that we all want; it is something that each of us needs. If you focus on your interactions with other people, you will undoubtedly see how many of your communications reflect this need, noticing how empowered you feel when you trust that you are worthwhile and how debilitating it can be when you don't feel this way.

〜 Elena

Depending on how you fared in your angering situation, your own estimation of your value—your self-esteem—may be even higher that it was before your upsetting experience. Such was the case with Elena, who became furious with a contractor when he carelessly caused further damage to her house and then tried to deny responsibility for the destruction. In her furious anger, Elena accomplished something she would not previously have thought possible: she discovered her strength. As a result, she established control of the relationship and felt empowered to closely monitor the contractor's work to its successful completion.

Though she had always been easily cowed in the past, Elena said that her confrontation with her contractor forced her to connect with her own inner strength. After that experience, she has had less need of the power boost of her anger. Now that she has found and claimed her innate personal power, she feels better able to access it calmly and as forcefully as needed.

What happened to Elena was that her successful use of anger in an altercation with someone larger and seemingly more powerful changed her belief about herself. Formerly believing that she couldn't be powerful enough in confrontational situations, she now realizes the falseness of that belief. On the contrary, Elena now has proof that she has enough personal power to approach life's unpleasant surprises with greater trust in her own capacity to meet and successfully deal with them. Trusting her newly discovered inner strength, she now feels free to consider difficult situations more calmly, bringing both more thought and more caring to the resolution of the problem.

Feeling Devalued

While Elena's experience corrected an old mistaken belief, raising her self-esteem in the process, many others have not had so fortunate an outcome. Thus, you might have found, as many people have, that becoming angry has had a devaluing effect on your self-esteem.

First, you might feel devalued as a result of what happened in the original angering experience, perhaps feeling overpowered, mistreated, or simply bested by someone else. Second, even if your anger helped you to succeed in your interchange with the other person, you might have devalued yourself in your own mind. You may believe that somehow you should have been strong enough or able enough to handle the situation successfully without the need for the power boost of your anger.

These kinds of negative self-judgments are typical of many people's reactions to an angering experience. In these very common situations, you need a way to reestablish your sense of personal worth so that you are certain of it in your own mind. Doing so after an upsetting experience is often key to working through and getting beyond that experience. In our culture, however, doing so can be difficult.

Culturally Learned Messages About Your Value

Our culture teaches confusing messages when it comes to self-validation. On the one hand, we are offered the ideal of an independent, self-confident achiever. The model we see in various movies, television programs, books, and news stories is of a single, strong-minded individual who acts according to his or her conscience, regardless of what others believe or expect. In the end, of course, this person is proven right and becomes the heroine or hero.

On the other hand, while we are taught that we should all aspire to being a champion, so much of what we all learn culturally gives us the subtle but pervasive message that instead of being a hero, we are continually at risk of not even being okay. We've all been taught over a lifetime of television, radio, magazines, and other media advertising that we are not enough, not okay—unless we buy the particular clothes, car, or myriad other products that advertisers wish to sell us. We have also been trained through repeated pharmaceutical ads that we will not be able to feel or perform optimally until we take yet another pill. What results is an ongoing struggle with the issue of self-esteem and an inclination to look outside for the answer rather than trusting ourselves. As we have seen, this inclination intensifies when an angry incident further shakes our self-esteem. When this happens, self-validation becomes a valuable and important step in reestablishing and anchoring our own sense of worth.

Valuing Yourself

You may be tempted, as so many are, to try to accomplish step three by telling your story to family members or friends whom you trust. We often do this in the hope that they will validate our conclusions about the rightness of our actions and the unfairness and wrongness of the other person's. You might be used to seeking outside corroboration rather than providing it for yourself. You might also want outside support to counter the mental image you may carry, in which you imagine that the offending person is telling others how he or she was right and *you* were wrong. After all, this other person has his or her own frame of reference, one that clearly conflicted with your own during the upsetting incident. As a result, you may want to know that others are on your side as an attempt to bolster belief in yourself. However, getting validated by someone else usually doesn't work well unless you already have high self-esteem. It's difficult to believe in the worth that others say you have if you don't already feel it within. As you have seen from previous examples, your frame of reference, constricted by your learned belief in the limitations of your own worth, would block the truth that others tell you. To really believe it, you have to validate yourself by acknowledging that, from your frame of reference at the time of the incident, *you were right*! Your thoughts, your feelings, and the actions you took were all correct.

By completing step three, you take back both your power and your responsibility for resolving the issue of self-esteem in the only way that truly works: affirming your own legitimacy and self-worth. Doing so can deepen your trust in yourself as it firmly connects you with your own authority. Then, feeling calmer and surer of yourself, you can use the incident to grow. You can become more curious about what happened, what you might learn from it, and how you might widen your frame of reference and proceed now that the event is part of your history. To the extent that you trust and value yourself, you can explore your experience openly and deeply so that you can, with the remaining steps, find the deeper understanding and freedom that inevitably await you.

What If You Don't Feel Completely Right?

Validate yourself honestly, expressing what you truly believe, whether it is that your thoughts, feelings, and behavior were 100 percent correct or that they were simply more on target than the other person's were. Life usually isn't completely clear—we rarely know anything with 100-percent certainty. You may find that you frequently do not feel completely blameless, but that you still feel a lot less blameworthy than the other person. Whether you feel completely in the right or only partially, simply validate your truth as you know it right now. What's important is that you state what you truly believe, including the fact that you did the best you could and that you feel unfairly treated. Then explain why and validate that explanation for yourself.

What If You're Eventually Proven Wrong?

Even more than wanting to be right, many people fear being wrong. Since we are all human, however, being wrong at times is a given. Recall a disagreement that left you sure you were right, and then you learned new facts that gave you new insights about the event. Perhaps this widening of your frame of reference gave you even more reassurance of the correctness of your stance. Perhaps it changed your mind. Or maybe it led you to decide that both you and the other person were somewhat right and somewhat wrong. Whatever the result, it occurred because your willingness to risk being wrong led to your continued exploration and to the new information this search brought to light. We all know that this is what happens in real life. We think we know the absolute truth, and then we learn more. Whether in science, medicine, philosophy, or personal relationships, "absolute" is not usually a working term. There is always more to learn.

It's not a loss if, on further exploration, you discover that you were mistaken. In fact, this discovery is actually a win because it will help set you free from the belief that caused the mistake. It is a success when you use your mistake as a catalyst for growth. Validating yourself in step three is both valid and valuable whether or not you change your mind later. In this step you are affirming that, given your frame of reference—given what you *currently* know—your behavior was correct. While future information may widen your frame and cause you to change your mind as a result of your increased awareness, you can only base your current conclusion on what you know at present. With this step, you align your thinking both with what is actually true (the fact that your actions were correct given what you knew) and with what allows for your human propensity for growth (the fact that you can use the strength you gain from this step to help you explore your experience more deeply and fully).

⫶⫶ Kristin

Kristin is the woman we met in step one who was angry with her uncooperative coworker, a woman who refused to do her share of the work. Kristin used what she called a "mental exercise" to complete step three. She began by clearly telling herself that, from her perspective, she was right. Then she took a breath and did a body scan, mentally bringing her focus up through her body, locating and acknowledging the surge of energy she received from taking her own side in the disagreement. It was feeling this surge of energy, she later explained, that let her know that she had finished this step. Taking her own side, telling herself that, from her frame of reference, she was unequivocally right, felt freeing to her. It increased her sense of energy and power.

Kristin reported that giving herself validation was a huge relief for her. She said that previous to doing this step, she had always assumed she was somehow wrong. Validating herself helped Kristin increase her inner sense of balance and steadiness. While she remained aware that she was affirming herself from her own limited, current frame of reference, she found that doing so was liberating. It released her from the rigidity of right versus wrong and allowed her the calming effect of acknowledging that she had done her human best and that, given what she currently knew, her beliefs and actions were correct.

⫶⫶⫶ Kirk

Kirk, as we read earlier, had worked his way up to the position of assistant manager before he was suddenly fired. Even though his boss told him that customers were complaining about him, Kirk suspected that the real reason for his firing was that his boss wanted to promote a newly hired friend.

After telling himself that he was right, Kirk wrote that statement into messages that he taped all over his apartment. Normally confident, he wanted to keep his self-esteem high, and he thought that reminding himself, over and over, that his firing was not his fault would accomplish that goal. It certainly did. Repeatedly seeing the messages all over his apartment helped strengthen his determination to use this experience as motivation to find a better job. As he took the remaining steps, he began thinking about what it was he really wanted to do and who, among the people he knew, might be helpful.

⫶⫶⫶ Jeff

Jeff was angry at his wife, Lila, because she had gotten so unfairly mad at him for picking her up late from work. While it was true that he had been late several times before, he had promised to change his behavior and be on time, and had done so for the last three days. Today, though, he was late again, and Lila had exploded at him. Thinking about what happened, he was sure he was the injured party. There had been an accident that had tied up traffic and, though he tried his best, he could not quite make it to Lila's workplace on time. "Okay," he told himself self-righteously, "there were plenty of other times when maybe I did deserve to be yelled at for being late—but not this time. It's not my fault that some idiot tied up the middle lanes and blocked traffic. I'm really trying to change. Lila should have understood and cut me some slack."

Jeff could see that Lila had reason to be angry at past behavior and, as a result, would be sensitive to his arriving late again. He gave her points for that. *Still*, he thought, validating himself, *this time I'm a lot more right than she is.* Jeff wrote his self-validation in his anger journal and then imagined Lila hugging him in agreement. Then he completed the remaining steps before talking things over with her.

EXERCISE: Giving Yourself Validation

This is a step best taken when you have the time to really focus on yourself in a space that is comfortable and quiet. You might consider including items that reflect self-love to you—perhaps plants, special flowers, or objects that are meaningful to you and that remind you of how special you are. If the details of your angering experience and your thoughts, feelings, and actions are not clear in your mind, take a few minutes to reread your self-discovery letter. Then, when you're ready, take the following steps.

Affirm yourself. Reassure yourself that your thoughts, feelings, and actions during that experience were correct. From your frame of reference at the time of the incident, you were right. As you affirm this truth to yourself, be sure to speak to yourself with all due respect, as you would to a valued friend. In fact, that is what you truly can be to yourself.

Write down your affirmation. Use your anger journal to record this affirmation so that you have it and can refer back to it. You can sign it, if you like, as part of a self-esteeming ceremony. If so, consider adding one or more of the following:

- Do a mental exercise (like Kristin did), visualizing your acknowledgment to yourself in your own personal way.

- Write your affirmation statement on pieces of paper and tape them where you'll be sure to see them often.

- Buy a special flower, plant, or some other object that pleases you, and place it in your home where you will often pass it. Then, each time you see it, this object will be a reminder of your validity and your worth.

- Imagine hugging yourself. Some people actually do hug themselves, and many have said that it feels wonderfully affirming and loving.

As you can see, there are a number of ways to complete this step. However you decide to do it, the more seriously and caringly you do so, the greater its healing effect.

At first, validating yourself may feel artificial and not believable. These feelings indicate that you're creating a new response that, with time and practice, can become both natural and automatic as you increase your ability to trust and befriend yourself. As this happens, you may feel your self-esteem rise as you firmly create an inner ground to stand on that will be much more difficult to shake, no matter what the future brings.

The Gift-of-Anger Process

Let's review the steps that we've examined so far, including step three. After you work to affirm yourself and your feelings and responses in your angering experience, you'll be ready to move on to step four—the heart of the process. The steps are:

1. **Recognize Your Anger...**

   Learn your:

   - Physical symptoms

   - Mental patterns

   - Associated feelings

   so that you can identify your most reliable personal anger cue.

   And Regain Your Emotional Balance

   Take private time to:

   - Breathe diaphragmatically

   - Take an exercise break

   - Talk it out

   - Write a poison-pen letter

   - Or use any other method that safely releases your adrenaline without causing harm, either to yourself or to anyone else

2. **Notice Your Thoughts and Feelings**

   - Describe the anger-provoking experience and your thoughts and feelings about it.

   - Write them out in a self-discovery letter.

3. **Give Yourself Validation**

   Acknowledge that from your current frame of reference, you are *right*!

   Now let's move to step four.

CHAPTER 7

Step Four: Identify Your Unmet Need

You have calmed yourself so that you can explore your experience. You've written your self-discovery letter and given yourself validation by affirming that, from your frame of reference at the time of the incident, your thoughts, feelings, and actions were correct. Now you're ready for the pivotal step in this transformative process. You are ready to identify your *unmet need*. What is your unmet need? It is where you'll find the cure for your painful feelings. It is the missing ingredient that can help you heal your pain and update your beliefs.

Writing out your thoughts and feelings in your self-discovery letter, you undoubtedly wrote about the painful feelings that your angering experience evoked. In this step, step four, you review those feelings and name their cure. Doing so, you will almost inevitably find that the cure you name is the meeting of a need that has been insufficiently met in your life.

Remember Valerie? She was angry with the other members of her church's program committee, feeling that their behavior toward her was unfair and disrespectful. When she reviewed her self-discovery letter, Valerie saw that she had written about feeling *ignored, minimized, dictated to,* and *invisible* when the other committee members dismissed her ideas without any discussion of their potential merits. When asked to name the cure for those painful feelings, she thought for a while and then said that the cure would be to be *seen* and *heard* by the other members of the committee. Feeling seen and heard, the opposite of what actually happened in her experience, are Valerie's unmet needs. They are also basic human needs that all of us have. Like Valerie, others have reported that the cure for their painful feelings lay in receiving enough of a basic, human need that was not sufficiently met by their experience. When you name the cure for your own hurtful feelings, you will most likely find that you, too, have named one of the many needs that must be met for all of us if we are to have a satisfying life.

The Cause and Effect of an Unmet Need

Unlike a *want*, something that you would enjoy having but is not necessary, a *need* is vital to your well-being. So, for instance, along with the needs to be seen and to be heard, love, belonging, respect from others, self-respect, understanding, compassion, and autonomy are all vital human needs. Other needs that clients have named include the need for friendship, intimacy, appreciation, acceptance, recognition, empathy, and being valued.

When you believe that one of these needs (or another need that you might name) has been incompletely met in your life, you feel a sense of deficiency in that area. You, like almost everyone else, have unmet needs, areas where you feel deficient. They are part of your human experience, part of what makes so many of us focus on personal growth.

There is no objective measure for how fully a need must be satisfied. We each decide for ourselves how much respect we must have in order for that need to be sufficiently met, how much love is enough, and how much autonomy feels right. When we believe we have received enough, we feel strong in that area, able to weather other people's potential inability to be caring of us in that particular way. When we believe a need to be insufficiently met, we not only feel deficient in that area, but we also become sensitive to whether or not others are meeting this need for us.

Like Valerie wanting the other committee members to really see and hear her, we all seek fulfillment of our unmet needs from others. As a result, we become sensitive to what we interpret as someone else either offering us what we need or withholding it from us. That sensitivity keeps us feeling somewhat separate and untrusting, as we hope for a positive interaction that will meet our need yet also feel potentially at risk of being wounded by the other person if they don't meet our need. Even if we're not fully conscious of it, some of our energy in each exchange will go into staying alert to the possibility of having our unmet need and those painful feelings attached to it reactivated by the other person's behavior.

If respect, for example, is one of your unmet needs, then having others respect you will be important to you. If so, when you believe yourself respected in a particular interaction, you will likely feel larger, stronger, and more important. On the other hand, if you believe that you have been disrespected in an interaction, you will likely be left feeling weaker and quite possibly angry in reaction.

However, if you've received enough respect in your life to make you feel confident in that area, you are more likely to stay calm and balanced no matter how the other person behaves. If they are respectful you might be glad, but you probably won't feel stronger or more important as a result. You already feel strong and important enough in that area. If the other person is disrespectful, you won't like that behavior and might wonder why he or she would act in a demeaning manner, but you are unlikely to need the power boost of anger. While you might wish for a more favorable attitude on the other person's part and dislike their actions, you will be more likely to recognize the person's behavior as stemming from their own issues. They have their own unmet needs that narrow and cloud their frame of reference, keeping them from seeing you accurately and clearly.

As an analogy, think about what would happen if you proudly showed someone a new, green sweater you had just bought, and instead of admiring it, the person said, "That's not green, it's red." Knowing your sweater to be green, you probably wouldn't become angry with this person. Instead, you would realize that they have a vision defect. They're probably color-blind, and one of the ways their particular blindness manifests is that they cannot accurately see the colors of other people's clothing. Their color blindness limits their frame of reference in a way that makes it impossible for them to satisfy your desire to have your sweater admired. They cannot accurately see your sweater, so they cannot fully admire it.

Now imagine that that same person insults you and you feel disrespected. Is it right for that person to insult you? No, of course not. A person may disagree with you or want you to change a behavior, but being personally insulting is disrespectful. Again, this person has a vision defect—only this time it is their "emotional vision" that is defective. Their own unmet needs are obscuring their perception, and they cannot see you fully and clearly. If you respond to their insult with anger, though, your behavior indicates that being respected is probably an unmet need of yours. Were that not the case, you would be much less likely to take the other person's words or actions personally. You would recognize that the problem is theirs.

⑾ Jim

Jim, a man we met earlier, who had been passed over for a promotion, felt betrayed and rejected. He identified his unmet need as the need for recognition. "I worked so hard," he said, "and then they gave the promotion to someone who hadn't worked nearly as hard as I had. That promotion meant a lot to me; not just the money, but the title, too—the recognition of all the work I've put in."

Looking more deeply at his need for recognition, Jim noticed a pattern emerging. "This has happened before," he said. "Actually, now that I think about it, I can remember being really young and getting angry because I felt that no one paid enough attention to me. Even when I worked really hard, I felt like nobody really noticed."

When you identify an unmet need, it will often feel familiar to you. While not everyone has this experience, many people, like Jim, have been able to trace their need back to a very early origin. That's because our needs remain active until they are satisfied, no matter how long that takes. They cause upset and anger until they are met.

While Jim may have been truly taken for granted by his boss, if he had felt sufficiently recognized in his life, he might have been able to respond by talking with his boss about his disappointment and discussing his career potential rather than reacting to his hurt feelings by immediately deciding to look for another job. In fact, rather than waiting for the recognition he hoped to get, he would possibly have talked with his boss as soon as he heard about the open position or even discussed his career ambitions when he was hired. What kept him from being able to do so was his strong need for recognition and his fear that, once again, his need might not be met. As a result, rather than being able to calmly discuss the situation with his boss, Jim fell into an old pattern of waiting to see what would happen and then becoming angry and deciding to end the relationship when he didn't like what occurred.

⑾ Linda

Linda was mad at her sister and her mom. It seemed like her sister was always caught up in some terrible problem, and Linda's mother was always tending to her. Furthermore, Linda's mom expected Linda to be the strong one in the family, the one who didn't have any problems.

"I'm so sick of the way they treat me. All my life my sister's been the needy one who's gotten all the attention. Why can't it ever be my turn?" Linda complained. "Why can't my mother ever ask me if *I* need anything? And why can't my sister just grow up?"

Linda said she felt left out. "Actually," she said sadly, "I've felt left out my whole life." She defined her unmet need as the need to belong and immediately identified the fact that her unmet need was part of a lifelong pattern. Like Jim in the earlier story, Linda was able to trace her feelings far back into childhood.

Like Linda and Jim, you have needs that will remain active until you have met them enough to feel satisfied. They will cause painful feelings and probably anger until they are met to the extent that you no longer feel lacking in this area. By identifying your unmet need, you are also identifying an area where you can heal and strengthen so that you will not be as vulnerable to unexpected events or to other people's behavior. You will be better able to see the situation more clearly, understand it more fully, and choose your response to it more objectively and successfully.

Beliefs, Feelings, and Needs

We've examined how beliefs and feelings affect your anger response in previous chapters, but the idea of an unmet need is new. Let's briefly review how it fits into what you have already learned and discuss what makes it key to understanding your anger and working with it productively.

You learned in chapter 3 that you formed many of your beliefs by hearing them stated emphatically and repeatedly as true, and that you learned some of your most deeply held beliefs when you were too young to realistically evaluate their messages. Some of those beliefs, often the ones that cause you the most pain and therefore trigger the most anger, are beliefs you've learned about yourself. These convictions most likely began as repeated statements by which others defined you, eventually becoming your own convictions about what kind of person you are. To name a few, they are beliefs about whether you are loveable or unlovable, capable or incapable, smart or stupid, acceptable or unacceptable, strong or weak, able to make friends easily or not, someone others respect or not, and someone who belongs or not.

Once you have learned a negative belief about yourself (and we all have), you have resulting painful feelings of inadequacy and hurt. Your need has not been sufficiently met in the area of your limiting belief. Consciously or unconsciously, you may even believe that your need cannot ever be sufficiently met in this area, because so often we simply accept as fact the identity we were given in our very early lives.

These painfully limiting beliefs, helping to form and constrict your frame of reference, will prevent you from seeing ways to meet your needs. Think back to Jim's limiting belief about recognition and how it kept him from even considering discussing his potential for promotion with his boss. Jim was locked in an ongoing pattern of disappointment and anger at some of the people and events in his life. His anger at being passed over for promotion was simply the latest example.

It can be hard to directly change a belief, not just because it's already established, but because it has often become so automatic that you may not even realize you have it. In fact, people often cannot identify their limiting and pain-inducing beliefs about themselves. What most people do realize, though, is the fact that they have painful feelings. Most of us can identify those. Once we do so, as you undoubtedly did in your self-discovery letter, our painful feelings can direct us to the cure for our pain. Labeling the cure—by labeling your unmet need—and then beginning to enact the cure will change your definition of yourself, because as you consciously grow in strength and ability to meet your needs, it will become obvious that those old limiting beliefs no longer fit.

So, to restate the path you are on, your painful feelings can direct you to their cure—meeting your unmet need. Labeling your unmet need in this chapter and beginning to meet it in the next chapter will lead to a positive change in your beliefs about yourself. As you meet your need to a greater and greater degree, you feel increasingly in touch with your own inherent strength in that area, the area where you once felt only weakness and deficiency.

By identifying and then meeting your need, you widen your frame of reference, actually becoming more than you used to be. Meeting this need will increase your awareness, strength, and sense of peace because you will be more in touch with your innate capacity to handle what life brings you. The power boost of your anger is important when you need it, but gaining the awareness, true strength, and peace that identifying and meeting your need brings is far more valuable and useful. Doing so can raise your self-esteem as it provides you with a capacity to handle life's inevitable ups and downs. Identifying and meeting your need does not mean that painful situations won't still occur. They will. What will become increasingly different is your definition of them. As your frame of reference widens, you become increasingly able to view them as unfortunate experiences that you can hold, deal with, and calmly move beyond.

Identifying Your Unmet Need

There are a variety of ways to identify your unmet need. A good one to start with is to reread your self-discovery letter and underline the painful feelings you wrote about, just as Valerie underlined feeling ignored, minimized, dictated to, and invisible. Then ask yourself what your cure would be. Valerie labeled her own cure as being seen and heard, the opposite of what she had experienced. Like Valerie, many people have found that their cures were the opposite of what they received from their upsetting experiences. You might find this to be true for you, too.

If you need more help, you might ask yourself what made you feel both unable to easily fix the problem and unable to tolerate it. You can also ask what made this experience different from other difficult experiences that did not result in your becoming angry. Then, to further understand your unmet need, you can ask questions to discern the pattern. For instance, you might ask yourself whether or not your underlying feelings and the unmet need you identified are familiar. If so, what is your history with them?

Your answers to these questions should clarify your need. You most likely will not have to answer all the questions, since they all ask the same thing in different ways. Start with one and, if you do not feel that answering it has sufficiently identified your need, try the others.

As in the previous step, writing your answers down in your anger journal will help you more clearly define your need and more thoroughly explore and understand it. Interestingly, though, this step is often best done when you're tired. If you carefully think through your answers before writing them, you are more likely to restrict yourself to writing what you already know and accept. If you write when you are too tired to censor your thoughts, you may well give yourself new information. You might try completing this step when you feel fresh, and again when you feel sleepy enough to have a hard time engaging your mind. Check the results against each other and, if they're different, see which fits you most.

Naming Your Need

In one of the examples we looked at earlier, Valerie named her needs to be seen and heard. As she did this, she noticed a release of emotion that felt like a sigh of relief as she realized that she had accurately named her unmet need. This was her cue that she had seen and heard herself clearly by interpreting her need accurately. Doing so, she released some of the energy still held in the upsetting experience and illustrated the fact that each of us expresses our own unmet needs uniquely, in a way that feels personally true.

Cindy, Janine, and Dan, for instance, all came for therapy after their marital partners left them. While they all expressed feeling both devastated and betrayed, Cindy identified her unmet need as the need to feel cherished, while Janine said she needed to feel valued and Dan said he needed to feel both loved and lovable. In all three of these similar examples, the unmet need was labeled differently, each person articulating his or her need in a way that felt personally correct. Each then expressed some relief at having accurately named their need.

Like Valerie, Cindy, Janine, and Dan, others have repeatedly reported a sense of relief and release resulting from accurately identifying their unmet need and labeling it in a way that best fit them. Doing so, they were able to see and label a part of themselves that, for some of the people, was surprising. For some, identifying their unmet need initiated the conscious reclaiming of a part of themselves that they hadn't focused on before. For others, consciously identifying their need acted as a reminder of an emotional area ready for healing and strengthening.

EXERCISE:
Identifying and Naming Your Unmet Need

Now that you understand more about identifying and naming your need, it's time to take this important step yourself. You can begin by opening your anger journal and turning to the pages that contain your self-discovery letter. Looking at your letter, take the following steps:

1. Underline the hurtful feelings that you listed in your letter and then ask yourself what the cure might be. Often it will be the opposite of the painful feeling, such as feeling appreciated if you felt unappreciated.

2. You can also ask yourself directly what you needed from the person or situation that you didn't get.

3. You might ask yourself what was missing that kept you from being able to calmly tolerate and deal with the problem. Or think about what hurt you the most and what you wish had happened instead.

To further help you identify your unmet need, consult the partial list of unmet needs below to see which fits best with your upsetting experience. You might recognize your need from this list, or the list may remind you of a need that fits your situation more accurately.

A Partial List of Unmet Needs

Acceptance	Love
Appreciation	Recognition
Autonomy	Respect
Belonging	Self-respect
Compassion	Understanding
Empathy	To be heard
Friendship	To be seen
Intimacy	To feel valued

So many people have said that taking the time to focus on their own need and label it in a way that felt accurate resulted in their feeling more seen and appreciated by themselves. None of them had yet taken steps to fill their need out in the world, but naming it in a way that felt personally true was a first and powerfully important self-healing act. I hope you feel the same.

The Gift-of-Anger Process

Now that you understand step four, let's review. Remember, identifying your unmet need is the core of this process, so give yourself the time and space to think about it until you feel satisfied. The steps are:

1. **Recognize Your Anger...**

   Learn your:

   ⍾ Physical symptoms

   ⍾ Mental patterns

   ⍾ Associated feelings

   so that you can identify your most reliable personal anger cue.

   And Regain Your Emotional Balance

   Take private time to:

   ⍾ Breathe diaphragmatically

   ⍾ Take an exercise break

   ⍾ Talk it out

   ⍾ Write a poison-pen letter

   ⍾ Or use any other method that safely releases your adrenaline without causing harm, either to yourself or to anyone else

2. **Notice Your Thoughts and Feelings**

   ⍾ Describe the anger-provoking experience and your thoughts and feelings about it.

〰 Write them out in a self-discovery letter.

3. Give Yourself Validation

Acknowledge that from your current frame of reference, you are *right*!

4. Identify Your Unmet Need

There are *always* unmet needs. These needs are *always valid.*

Next, we'll discuss meeting your need in step five.

CHAPTER 8

Step Five: Take Action to Meet Your Need

Having identified your unmet need, you are now ready to meet it. Yes, you *can* meet your need! This chapter shows you how. You will also learn how to anchor your positive changes so that they become part of who you are and affect your responses in similar, future situations. You will find examples of how other people accomplished this step and learn how to personalize it effectively.

As you take the insights you have gained through the first four steps of this process and translate them into healing and strengthening actions with this step, you will naturally increase your trust in your ability to manage adversity successfully. You have come through the devaluing experience and are becoming a stronger and more capable person as a result. Just as the angering experience may have shaken your self-esteem, taking steps to meet your unmet need can restore your sense of self, even raising it to a higher level than it was before the upsetting experience.

Taking steps to meet your need will not change the factual reality of a difficult experience, but it will definitely affect how you're able to interpret the experience and respond to it. As you move toward meeting your need, the negative experience you had becomes manageable. Of course, this doesn't make it an experience you either wanted or approve of, but now you can deal with it.

Guidelines for Meeting Your Need

When you're ready to meet your need, there are four guidelines to follow. These simple guides will help you focus clearly on how to successfully complete this step.

Decide Who Will Participate

The first guideline for meeting your unmet need is to decide whether or not to involve the person with whom you were angry. It can be wonderful to work through the problem with the other person, to feel that your needs have been met and your relationship has been strengthened in the process. It can be great, but it is not necessary. In fact, sometimes it's impossible. You may, for instance, be unwilling or unable to involve the other person directly. Perhaps the other person is not interested in working through the problem with you; maybe it wouldn't be appropriate to approach the person in this way. No matter the reason, you can still meet your identified need because doing so does not necessitate the cooperation of the person with whom you were angry. It simply takes staying true to what is important to you as you develop a plan that fits you and then follow it.

Clarify Your Goal

The second guideline for meeting your unmet need is to consider how you will know when your need is sufficiently met. How will your life look and be different? For instance, if your unmet need is for respect, how will you know when you have enough respect? You might imagine that you would feel respected enough only if everyone shows you respect, but that happening is unlikely. Life is almost never one way, 100 percent, and we usually don't expect it to be. Having your need met sufficiently and in a way that is important to you is what matters, and only you can decide what that looks like. You can be thinking about this as, later in this chapter, you read examples of others who identified and took steps to meet their own needs.

Take Small, Manageable Actions

The third guideline is to take small, manageable actions toward meeting your need. So many of us want to change quickly so that we can swiftly rid ourselves of discomfort. However, we humans aren't designed to make fast changes. When you try to make a significant behavioral change quickly, you greatly increase your likelihood of failure. Failing, you heighten your chances of losing faith in your ability to succeed. It is a recipe for staying stuck, a recipe too many people follow.

Our world is so often focused on instant results. Everything from fast food to text messaging entices us with the notion of immediate gratification. And achieving quick results becomes an especially attractive goal when we are in pain. We want our discomfort to stop *now*. For change to happen and to last, however, you must move slowly so that you have time to integrate the change. It's important to take small steps that you can easily manage and then to congratulate yourself after confirming that you have successfully completed each small, manageable action.

Congratulate Yourself

The fourth and final guideline is to congratulate yourself honestly and sincerely after each small, manageable step you take toward meeting your need. This step is crucial because the act of self-congratulation serves to acknowledge the work you have completed and the resulting gains that you've made. Acknowledging each accomplishment helps update your beliefs about yourself as it cements the positive changes you're making with each step of growth. Congratulating yourself reminds you of the person you are becoming as a result of your hard work. Doing so attests to the fact that you have already become more than you were and that with each next new step you are continuing to become more aware, more emotionally strong, and more at peace with yourself and the world around you.

Sincerely complimenting yourself for each successfully completed action also gives you energy for taking the next action. Rather than possibly feeling demoralized by seeing your goal as unattainably distant (as many feel when first contemplating meeting their need), you will most likely find that your justifiable and sincere congratulations energize and invigorate you. Thus, moving toward your goal can increasingly become a positive experience—and perhaps even fun.

⅊ Dan

Dan's wife left him after a few years of marriage. Labeling his underlying painful feelings as devastation and betrayal, Dan identified his unmet needs to feel both loved and lovable. Noticing how intertwined his needs were, he decided to focus on his need to feel loved.

When I asked how he would know when he had met his need, Dan's answer was twofold. First, he said that when he had met his need sufficiently, he would better understand how to build a lasting relationship. Second, he said he would have a relationship in which he felt loved. These answers provided Dan with the direction he needed to begin formulating the first small, manageable actions he would take toward meeting his need.

"I want to understand what went wrong in my marriage," he said. "I want to know my part so I don't do it again." So, for his first small step, Dan listed the action of talking with his wife to get her perspective. Then he thought about how hard it might be for him to achieve this step. As a result, he broke this action down into several smaller, much more manageable ones. These included a seminar in nondefensive communication offered through his workplace and practice sessions with others in the class. He also wrote a good-bye letter to his wife, but this wasn't a letter he sent. Instead, it became the basis for several therapy sessions as Dan worked with the feelings that writing his letter brought up. His actions also included role-playing in his therapy sessions so that he could become more comfortable with the idea of having the conversation with his wife. In fact, as he broke his process into smaller actions sized to his own comfort level, it took quite a while before Dan actually asked his wife for her perspective.

Dan gave himself all the time he needed so that when he did ask for her viewpoint, he was able to do so without projecting blame and recrimination. His wife, as a result, was able to answer sincerely but gently. This conversation didn't repair the marriage, but it provided some healing for them both. It also gave Dan some important information about how his wife had seen him and their relationship.

Dan's second goal was to identify and act upon ways to widen his social circle by making satisfying connections with other people. Doing so, he decided, would give him the best opportunity to develop the close relationships that might lead to love. At this point he understood the importance of the size of each action he took, so he made sure that each one was small and manageable. He chose three to begin with.

Dan had lost many of his friends in the separation from his wife, so meeting potential new friends was an important goal. The first two actions Dan chose were to identify two recreational pastimes that he enjoyed or thought he might like to try. He had swum competitively in college, so he decided to begin swimming again. Then, thinking about how out of shape he felt, he listed joining a gym. Dan's third action was to locate the gyms in his area that also had a pool, a step made very easy by using his phone book and making a few phone calls.

Dan decided to keep a *success diary*, a separate diary devoted to recording each successful action he took and appreciating himself in writing for each one. Still, Dan's goal of feeling loved was a profound one, and at first he despaired of ever reaching it. Then, as he continued taking small, manageable actions and congratulating himself in writing with each success, he slowly began to notice a change. "I take myself more seriously now," he said eventually. "I'm developing a closer relationship with the most unlikely person—myself."

Dan had learned the most important truth of this step: whatever you hope for from others, be sure you're giving it to yourself. You are the model. Meet your need within yourself, and you are much more likely to get it met out in the world.

Had Dan not moved toward a closer, more loving relationship with himself, he might never have found it with another person because he would have been less likely to believe or trust another's love. Not meeting your own need makes it much harder to see and receive what you long for when someone else offers you the thing you need. Meeting your unmet need is first and foremost an inside job. It has to start with you.

At first Dan was concerned that focusing on meeting his own need would make him self-centered. What he came to realize, though, is that the opposite is true. Truly caring about himself necessarily included caring about others, because sharing loving and supportive relationships with others is usually a primary requisite for living a healthy and satisfying life. Too many people are in relationships in which one of them is sacrificed for the well-being of the other. But as Dan eventually realized, that kind of union simply creates unmet needs. Dan had tried so hard to please his wife that he had left himself out of the equation, and eventually, so did his wife. "The next time I find a partner," he said after completing a number of small, manageable actions, "I'll focus on us both."

⑾ Linda

We met Linda in chapter 7 and learned that she was angry with her mom for always focusing on her sister and angry with her sister for always being weak and needy. Linda said that she didn't want to involve either her mother or her sister in working through her anger. She didn't believe they would listen, and she wanted to avoid another family argument. She just wanted to do what she could to meet her unmet need on her own.

Linda felt left out of her family and defined her unmet need as the need to feel that she belonged. Asked how she treated herself, she admitted that in some ways she was no better at focusing on herself and including her own needs than her mother and sister were. "I guess I treat myself the way they treat me," she said finally. "I always expect myself to be strong and handle things."

Linda was surprised by this realization, and her answer to how she would know when she belonged surprised her as well. "I don't really expect my mom or my sister to change," she said. "They've been this way forever. But *I* want to change. I want to really accept myself, to appreciate myself, without demanding that I think, feel, or behave in any certain way. It's what I always wanted from my mom and sister. Maybe I'll never get it from them, but I do want it from me."

Linda's first small, manageable action was to complete a written exercise that would help her identify how she would behave differently if she were to truly recognize and appreciate herself. The exercise was simple and took about half an hour. On the top of a blank sheet of paper, she wrote, "If I really accepted myself and appreciated myself without demanding that I think, feel, or behave in any certain way, I would..." Then she used the rest of the space to complete the sentence in ways that would acknowledge the parts of her that had felt squelched and left out.

Her second action was to identify the item from that list that most interested her. In Linda's case, she identified taking a class in weaving. She smiled as she explained that she had always wanted to learn to weave yet had stopped herself, feeling that it would be frivolous and impractical to take the time.

Sometimes we discover surprising things when we stop pushing ourselves to be the person we are *supposed* to be. Listening at a deep, internal level, we give ourselves unexpected answers. It would have made logical sense for Linda's list to focus on asking others for help rather than always being strong. Instead, her list centered on activities that she had never allowed herself the freedom to pursue.

As a third action, Linda immediately wanted to commit to taking a weaving class. However, reminded of the importance of small, manageable steps, she decided instead that her third action would be to call her local art center and inquire about weaving classes.

It can be hard, especially at first, to make your commitments small and manageable enough to guarantee their accomplishment. It can be hard, but it is important. These commitments are promises that you make to yourself. Break the promise and you diminish your trust in yourself, making it harder to trust yourself the next time you try. By agreeing to small actions that you can take easily, you help ensure that you can comfortably keep your promise, increasing your faith in yourself and expanding your sense of empowerment each time you do so.

At first, Linda consciously told herself that she had done well as she completed each small step. After a while, she noticed that she was congratulating herself spontaneously as she finished taking each of her actions. She said she looked forward to the feeling of delight that would fill her each time she acknowledged herself this way.

⫶ Janet

Janet, whom we met in chapter 4, reported that she felt belittled and ignored by her primary-care physician, who misdiagnosed her symptoms and downplayed her pain. Even though many subsequent doctors had made the same mistaken diagnosis, Janet still blamed this doctor, feeling that after all her years of coming to him, he should have known her better and taken her complaints more seriously. Exploring her unmet need in step four, Janet described her need to feel understood. For step five, she said that she wanted to meet her need by having her doctor understand her. "I don't want him to just listen to me perfunctorily," she said. "I want him to take the time to truly understand me."

Looking back, Janet could see that she had given her doctor so much authority that she had accepted his diagnosis and not argued when he dismissed her pain, even though she thought he was incorrect. Now, she decided that one way to meet her unmet need was to talk with her doctor again and tell him how she had felt at her last appointment with him.

Janet wanted to do as much as she could to ensure a successful appointment, one in which her doctor both listened to her and understood how she felt, but she was also realistic. "I'll know this meeting was a success if I can say how I really feel. Then, if he apologizes, that's great. I can continue to be his patient," she said. "And if he doesn't, I'll find another doctor." With her goal clearly in mind, she focused on steps to take before scheduling her appointment. "I have two steps," she said.

Janet's first step was to clear away more of her anger so that her emotions would not put her doctor on the defensive. The second step was to decide what she wanted to say in her meeting. Reviewing those steps, Janet realized that they were each far too large to easily accomplish, so she broke each one down into several smaller steps.

In order to clear away more of her anger, Janet repeated the gift-of-anger process, taking one small, manageable step at a time and congratulating herself as she completed each one. She then took several actions involving journaling and rehearsal in order to become more certain about what she wanted to say to her doctor. She used some therapy sessions for these steps and practiced with her husband, as well.

Janet began complimenting herself after each small successful action, and after a while, she began to make her self-acknowledgments fun by leaving herself congratulatory phone messages on her home phone. She would then enjoy listening to the messages that evening. Eventually she began saving the messages on her phone so that whenever she needed a reminder, she could play a number of them and notice the many steps she had already taken and the stronger, more capable person she was becoming.

As a result of taking the time to truly understand her need, translate it into a goal, and follow through on her commitment to herself, Janet was able to talk to her doctor clearly and concisely. "I think he really understood his mistake," she said, "and he said he understood my feelings, as well. And then he apologized."

Anger cannot provide a way to alter or negate the reality of what has happened, but it can lead you to become aware of how to work creatively and beneficially with the new reality that the experience has brought about. Thus, not only did Janet improve communication with her doctor, she also learned to support her own well-being by asking timely questions and by disagreeing if she thought her doctor was in error. Doing her own inner work and learning her own lessons, Janet was able to keep her doctor and gain better service from him as well.

EXERCISE: Creating Your Own Action Plan

Now that you've learned how to take small, manageable actions to meet your need and have read about others who have successfully done so, it's time to create your own action plan. The following directions will guide you:

1. To begin creating an action plan of your own, look at the unmet need you identified in chapter 7. If you identified more than one need, pick the one that seems most important to you and write that need at the top of a sheet of paper.

2. Now, consider how you'll know when you have met your need. How will your life look and be different? Answering this question establishes a way to tell when you have met your need and also often suggests a pathway toward it.

3. With your goal more clearly defined, write down three small, manageable actions you can take to start you on your way toward it. It may well take many actions to actually satisfy your need; however, these first three steps will begin moving you toward your goal. If you can't think of three actions to take, just write down one or two. It's the commitment and follow-through that are important,

and committing and following through on one or two actions will make it easier to think of others that will help you reach your goal.

As you complete this exercise, remember that the guideline for choosing your first three actions is to be sure to make each one small enough to be very easily achieved. Then, as you complete each action, congratulate yourself sincerely. When you've accomplished the actions you listed, decide on your next three small, manageable actions.

EXERCISE: An Alternative Action Plan

If you have a difficult time creating your action plan, either because you can't think of any actions or because it's hard to break your actions down enough for you to accomplish them easily and successfully, try the following exercise:

1. With your goal firmly in mind, write it at the top of a blank sheet of paper.

2. Underneath your goal, list all of the actions that you can think of that are necessary to reach it.

3. Put the actions in order by placing a number 1 before the action that must be taken first and ranking the rest with consecutive numbers in order of their timing.

4. Now, turn you paper over and write your number-one action at the top of the page.

5. Think about what actions might be necessary to complete this first objective and list them underneath it, ranking them as well. You will now have ideas for actions to take on one side of the paper and the action that must be taken first, broken down into smaller, more manageable actions, on the second side of the paper.

6. Looking at the second side of the paper, decide whether or not the top three actions are small enough to complete easily and successfully. If so, those are your first three small, manageable actions. If not, take another sheet of paper and write the first small action at the top and then list what needs to happen to complete it. Continue this process until you have three very manageable actions that you know you can complete easily and successfully. Complete those three, congratulating yourself after each action. Then go back to your list and choose the next three.

Widening Your Frame of Reference

When Janet talked to me about doing this step of the gift-of-anger process, she admitted that this one had felt really cumbersome at first. Then she began noticing that with each small, manageable accomplishment, her painful feelings felt a bit less painful and her old beliefs about herself slowly changed. Janet's frame of reference widened as a result of the accumulation of small actions she took. She became clearer about who she was and more confident about the stronger, more aware and capable person she was becoming. No longer caught and held fast in the habitual responses of her past, she felt a greater freedom to consider and act on her own needs and more able to remember that the people around her had their own needs, which might keep them from seeing her clearly and responding to her in the way she hoped. With her beliefs updated and her frame of reference thus widened, Janet became a better advocate for herself as well as more understanding of others.

Janet's story has a happy ending, but even if her doctor hadn't been able to hear what she was saying and apologize, her story still would have ended well. No matter what his response, Janet had gained a better understanding of her own need and was committed to getting it met. Had she not felt that her doctor comprehended what she was saying and would take her complaints seriously in the future, Janet would have done the research needed to find the kind of doctor who would.

Just as Janet, Linda, and Dan came to see, widening your frame of reference by making inner changes can have a positive and powerful effect on your life. Opening your perspective this way changes how you define yourself as you take actions to meet your needs and gain the sense of empowerment and well-being that comes as a result. You might not achieve your original goal, as Janet did when her doctor apologized, but consistently taking small steps to lessen your pain, update your beliefs, and become more of the person you have the innate capacity to be increases your ability to more calmly hold your experience rather than letting it continue to grab onto you. The experience then becomes part of your history—perhaps a significant part—but still one that you can acknowledge, learn from, and leave in the past. Taking actions to meet your needs and reaching more of your capacity as a result can open doors for you that you may not have even considered possible.

Make It Fun and Make It Yours

As you complete each step, you might simply congratulate yourself mentally, or you might do something as concrete as keeping a success diary. You might give yourself something special or do something you've always wanted to do. For more ideas, you might reread the "Giving Yourself Validation" exercise in chapter 6. On the other hand, you might come up with your own personal method of self-acknowledgment, one that's different from any of the ones mentioned in this book. The act of honoring your successes is an acknowledgment and a reward. It is something to enjoy. Have a good time with it!

EXERCISE: Choosing Your Reward

I hope you have some fun with the following exercise. It's meant to be a special treat to acknowledge your effort, your success, and your commitment to yourself. The two steps are to:

1. Make a list of some of the potential ways that you can acknowledge yourself as you complete each small, manageable action toward

your goal. This list could include anything from simply and sincerely complimenting yourself to gifting yourself with something you've been wanting. Consider everything from a sincere affirmation, to a call to a friend, to an ice cream cone, to dinner out. Whatever you think of as a reward can go on this list. Make your list as long as possible so you will have a lot of acknowledgements to choose from.

2.   Choose the three methods you will use to acknowledge yourself as you complete your first three small, manageable actions. You can use the same method each time or acknowledge yourself in unique ways each time. This is serious business...and it's also a time to have fun.

The Gift-of-Anger Process

Let's review the steps we've examined so far. Remember, you can always come back to these lists if you need a reminder of what makes up each step in the gift-of-anger process. The steps are:

1.   Recognize Your Anger...

Learn your:

- ⑾ Physical symptoms

- ⑾ Mental patterns

- ⑾ Associated feelings

so that you can identify your most reliable personal anger cue.

And Regain Your Emotional Balance

Take private time to:

- ⑾ Breathe diaphragmatically

- Take an exercise break

- Talk it out

- Write a poison-pen letter

- Or use any other method that safely releases your adrenaline without causing harm, either to yourself or to anyone else.

2. **Notice Your Thoughts and Feelings**

- Describe the anger-provoking experience and your thoughts and feelings about it.

- Write them out in a self-discovery letter.

3. **Give Yourself Validation**

Acknowledge that from your current frame of reference, you are *right*!

4. **Identify Your Unmet Need**

There are *always* unmet needs. These needs are *always valid*.

5. **Take Action to Meet Your Need**

- Decide how you will fill your need, and take small, manageable steps to do so.

- Congratulate yourself after each step.

CHAPTER 9

Step Six: Explore the Other Person's Frame of Reference

When you have completed enough small, manageable actions toward meeting your need and have acknowledged your successes sufficiently to notice a positive change in your self-esteem, then you're ready for step six. This step involves exploring the other person's frame of reference in order to get a sense of the unmet need that may have caused them to act as they did. Taking this step becomes possible only after you've made enough progress toward meeting your own need that you have gained the inner strength and objectivity necessary to consider the other person's unmet need, too.

Why Do It?

This is the point in learning about the gift-of-anger process where some people become angry at the process itself. In one of my workshops, an attendee named Kevin said adamently, "I was with you up to this point, but I'm not going any farther. I have no interest in understanding the frame of reference of the guy who hurt me. He doesn't deserve it and I won't give that to him!" Many people in workshops have at first echoed Kevin's sentiment. They did so until learning the important reasons to complete this step.

First, until you better understand the constricted frame of reference of the other person and acknowledge that he or she was unable to truly see you, you will continue to view that person narrowly. To you, they will remain an enemy, or at least a problem, rather than a whole human being. Why should this matter? Because by viewing the person solely as a problem, you are likely to stay locked into a level of anger and resentment toward them as life repeatedly brings you memories and experiences that remind you of this person's hurtful behavior. Caught in this repetitious cycle, you risk continually reinjecting yourself with anger—the very emotion you're trying to move beyond. It may be surprising that understanding the other person can be a necessary step in freeing yourself from your own anger, but that is the case.

The power of anger comes from its narrowed focus, from the blinders it puts on your vision so that you can't see the whole of the person you're angry at. All you can see is their injurious behavior. Take the blinders off by completing this step and you make room for the other person, for their difficulties as well as their shortcomings. With this widening focus, this increased ability to see the other person, your anger is much more likely to dissipate.

None of what you find will necessarily lead you to condone the other person's act, but that isn't the purpose of this step. The purpose of this step is to build on your earlier work to further free you from your pain and continue to increase your awareness. You gain your increased freedom and awareness as you realize that what occurred had much more to do with the other person and their needs and limitations than it did with you and yours. With this step, you can realize that, just as your anger narrowed your view of the other person, so their unmet need narrowed their view of you. Stuck in their own limited frame of reference, they were unable to fully see and appreciate you.

We don't hurt those whom we can truly see, and we do not truly see those whom we hurt. This maxim is a strong reason for taking this step. As you continue to widen your frame of reference by completing step six, you will become less likely to take someone else's comments or behavior personally. You'll become better able to acknowledge that, as with color blindness, the other person was at least temporarily blinded by an unmet need of their own. Understanding, you become more likely to be able to bring your problem-solving skills, your creativity, and perhaps even your compassion to the resolution of the problematic experience.

A second important reason for taking this step is that doing so is personally empowering. Just as the angering experience may have left you feeling weaker and perhaps seeing the other person as stronger, this step provides an opportunity to reempower yourself by better understanding the other person and what his or her limitations might be. In fact, if you refuse to take this step, you are actually denying your own power and magnifying the other person's. Refusal means saying that the person who angered you has the strength to keep you stuck in a negative experience and to block the wisdom and growth that seeing that person more fully inevitably brings you. This wisdom and growth are being held hostage by your belief that the other person already sees you fully and has hurt you beyond your ability to contain the event and move ahead with your life. When you make the experience more understandable by exploring the other's limitations, you act to create your own growth. You become better able to comprehend the event, to hold it emotionally rather than continuing to feel knocked over by it, and to hasten your progress in successfully moving beyond it.

Your Timing Is Important

For every person who says they will not complete step six, there is likely to be someone who cannot wait to do so. Jumping too quickly to repeat the process from the other's frame of reference, however, is as problematic as refusing to do so at all. While refusing to take this step may keep you stuck in anger, doing it too quickly may disconnect you from your feelings.

Terri, in another workshop, exemplified someone who was more comfortable moving quickly toward understanding the other person's frame of reference. Exploring her wish to move quickly to this step, Terri noted that she had been trained to focus on being compassionate and forgiving. Continuing to explore her feelings, she admitted, "I don't want to see how much I hurt. It's too painful."

Terri's feelings were an important reminder to pay attention to any discomfort and seek its meaning rather than immediately moving away from it. If what you are uncovering feels too painful, that's your cue to move more slowly and, if needed, seek a professional's help.

Done attentively, this process can restore and further your self-esteem and your ability to bring a growing sense of calm capacity to your handling of the events in your life. It can help you to be present with more of your life experiences without needing the power boost of your anger. What aids your success immeasurably is paying attention to your own feelings.

For Kevin, the man who initially refused to take this step, listening to his own feelings would mean staying with step five by continuing to take small, manageable actions toward satisfying his unmet need. By doing so, by being true to himself this way, Kevin will inevitably reach the point where he wonders about the other person. Meeting his own need sufficiently will engender his curiosity and his need to understand the other person. It will happen, as it has with so many others, when he has taken enough small, manageable steps to increase his emotional strength. Then he can more comfortably allow the inclusion of a more objective focus on someone with whom he is angry.

For someone like Terri, who wanted to rush into doing this step, paying attention to her feelings means focusing on the pain she is feeling and exploring what is causing it, perhaps by writing about it in her journal. More clearly identifying her pain and seeing how much she hurts, she might break her step-five actions into even smaller and more manageable steps. That way, she can accomplish them comfortably and watch her own sense of inner strength and capacity increase accordingly. Doing so, she will eventually be able to more objectively consider the person with whom she was angry—not as an escape from self-focus or as a behavior she "should" do, but from an inner readiness to do so.

This is a step to take after you've regained a sense of equilibrium by meeting enough of your unmet needs. How will *you* know when it's time? You'll know because attempting to begin the step before you're truly ready and willing invariably brings resentment rather than clarity, whereas hurrying to begin simply to stop your focus on yourself results in a lack of self-connection. Either is a trustworthy cue that it is not yet time for this step.

Paying attention to your feelings will more deeply and fully connect you with yourself and immeasurably further your ability to meet your own needs. Eventually, as you do this work, you will *want* to better understand the other person's actions. This understanding will help you widen your frame of reference so that you can more easily comprehend and contain the experience, finish resolving your feelings about it, and move more confidently ahead with your life.

How to Complete Step Six

You have been broadening your frame of reference with each step in this process, and with each incremental expansion, you may have noticed that you can hold your experience a bit more comfortably. Now your goal is to further increase your capacity to calmly hold the experience by understanding the other person as much as possible. This way you can see potential causes for his or her actions.

You can begin this step by thinking about what might have been going on for the other person five minutes before the incident. Ask yourself what might have contributed to the person's problematic behavior. For instance, did the other person look tired or frustrated right before your encounter? Did it seem like something difficult had just happened in his or her life? Or did they seem to be defensive, impatient, overwhelmed, or angry at something or someone else? Then, if you don't yet have enough of an answer to understand their behavior, ask yourself what might have been going on in the other person's life an hour before the incident. What about a year before the incident? A whole lifetime before the incident? Answer the questions with as much detail as possible so that you begin to see what might have caused their actions.

While you may know the answers to some of these questions, you will most likely be unable to answer many of them with any assurance of accuracy. Unless you know the person well, there will certainly be many blanks in your knowledge of him or her. With this step, however, even imagining what the other person may be experiencing can be of great value.

Everyone's choice of behavior is greatly impacted by training, learned beliefs, and the resulting unmet needs, as well as both distant and recent experiences. Imagining what at least some of those might be will help you see the person's immediate, hurtful actions as a piece of a larger picture, one in which what they said or did becomes more understandable to you. If you don't know the answer for sure, use as much of the truth as you are aware of, and then guess or use your imagination to explore potential personal issues that might have resulted in the other person's actions.

While you can write down your observations and conjectures in your journal if you wish, with this step you don't need to do so. You can simply give yourself time to think through your answers to the questions, imagining the answers when necessary. As you do, you will begin to understand that the person with whom you are angry can see you only through the filter of their current frame of reference, which is unavoidably constricted by their own unmet needs. As an example of someone who discovered this truth, consider Linda.

⑈ Linda

We met Linda in an earlier chapter when she complained that her mother focused all of her caring and attention on Linda's younger sister. Linda was angry with her mother for refusing to believe Linda might need help too, often referring to Linda as "the strong, capable one." Linda was also angry with her sister for being so constantly weak and needy rather than "growing up and becoming an adult like I had to do."

Reaching this step in the process, Linda decided to focus on her mother first. Thinking through her issue with her mom and realizing that it was a long-term problem rather than one pertaining only to a recent event, Linda reviewed as much as she knew of her mother's history. She began by asking herself what might have happened in her mother's life to make her consistently see Linda as strong and her sister as weak rather than bringing more balance to her view of each of her children.

The first realization Linda had was that her mother had been expected to be the strong one in her own generation.

She realized this as she remembered that her uncle was a very needy man, unable to successfully manage his life without constant aid from both his mother and his sister. "He was even worse than *my* sister," Linda acknowledged.

Asked about her grandmother, Linda remembered that her grandfather had had multiple sclerosis, so her grandmother had gotten a job and worked to support the family while also raising the kids. So her grandmother also had had to be the strong one.

Linda had known this information, but before focusing specifically on her family history she hadn't really thought about the repercussions of the situation. Doing so now, she said, "Now I really want to change. I didn't realize that this is a family pattern. I have two young children and I don't want to pass this pattern on to them."

We can only do what we've learned to do, so negative patterns often get handed down from generation to generation. The repetition continues until eventually, hopefully, a *chain breaker* is born. A chain breaker is someone who is conscious enough to recognize a hurtful pattern and strong enough to refuse to pass it on. When I told Linda that she was a chain breaker, she loved the idea. She said it made her feel both courageous and special.

Next, Linda decided to explore her mother's life in greater detail. She set aside an hour to imagine what her mother's life might have been like growing up in Linda's grandmother's house. Doing so reaffirmed her image of her mother as the strong one and her uncle as the weak one. As a result, Linda realized that rather than willfully refusing to see Linda accurately, her mother was unable to do so. Without having learned to recognize and grow beyond her own pattern of expecting herself to be strong, she simply couldn't recognize the hurt caused by passing this pattern on to her daughter. Stuck in her own limiting frame of reference, she could not truly see Linda.

"It's not her fault,' Linda said. "She's stuck. I always thought she just didn't love me as much as she loves my sister, but now I realize that it has nothing to do with love. Mom probably believes I'm just like her—the strong one."

Coupled with the small, manageable actions Linda had been taking in step five to meet her own need and improve her relationship with herself, this realization initiated a change in Linda's relationship with her mother. While she had been seeing her mother infrequently, mainly at family gatherings, Linda now began occasionally asking her mother to lunch. Linda began really listening when her mother spoke—not listening critically, but listening to learn more about her mom. Doing so, Linda sometimes found herself responding to her mother in an unselfconsciously loving way. As she did that more frequently, Linda began to notice something totally unexpected. Her mother was beginning to respond to Linda in the same unselfconsciously loving way.

We all long to be seen and appreciated. We all long for love. Taught to look for it from others, most people forget that it begins within. By beginning to satisfy our own unmet needs in step five and then adding an understanding of the other person's limited frame of reference, we help ourselves remember that we truly are more than we had thought. We're both stronger and more able to get our needs met than our narrow frame of reference had allowed us to believe. As well, we see that the other person is not as powerful as we made them out to be. In fact, they are stuck in a debilitating pattern caused by their own limited frame. They are simply doing the best they can, given their impaired vision.

As we take our own steps and increase our love and appreciation for ourselves, we have less need to be taken care of by others. Depending on the value we place on the relationship, we may become more willing to accept and appreciate the other person without trying to change him or her. Sometimes when this happens, just as with Linda's mother, the other person begins to make positive changes toward us, as well. This is not something to count on—but what a lovely surprise when it occurs!

We end Linda's story by noting that she eventually redid some of the steps she had used to increase her understanding of her mother, this time focusing on her sister. Predictably, Linda's relationship with her sister improved. What surprised

Linda, though, was the day her sister expressed her admiration for Linda and said she wanted to be more like her.

⑪ Kristin

In an earlier chapter, when Kristin was just beginning the gift-of-anger process, she described her coworker as a lazy, selfish person who refused to work harder than the bare minimum. Kristin said her colleague just wanted to "cheat the system," to get away with as much as she could. In Kristin's eyes, her coworker was laughing at people who worked hard at their jobs. She was laughing at Kristin.

Kristin's boss wasn't interested in hearing Kristin's complaints, and Kristin couldn't afford to leave her job. She was stuck with the upsetting situation and came to therapy in hopes of gaining help to move beyond her anger.

Contemplating viewing the world from her coworker's frame of reference, Kristin found herself resistant. So she decided to go back to step five and take more small, manageable actions toward meeting her own need before starting this step. Having done so, she was ready to proceed with viewing the world through her coworker's eyes. She explained that taking further actions to meet her own need helped make step six feel like a more natural outgrowth of her process rather than a step she would have to force herself to complete.

While she didn't have enough information to accurately explain her coworker's frame of reference, Kristin found herself able to imagine what her coworker might say. She picked a quiet time at home, closed her eyes, and imagined her coworker standing before her. In Kristin's imagination, her coworker began to speak about her job. She talked about having no more energy for work, of not being able to muster any more interest in the job she had held for so long. She spoke of feeling stuck, both unable to derive enjoyment from her current job and unable to find a new one. She said she was just trying to survive, trying to get by as best as she could.

Were these her coworker's true feelings? Kristin had no way of knowing for sure. What she did know was that it seemed possible, given the other person's length of time in that job and her frequent look of what Kristin interpreted as boredom.

Having this imaginary conversation helped Kristin to detach emotionally from her previously angry focus on her colleague. She could do so because she was newly able to imagine some plausible reasons for her colleague's negative behavior, reasons that had nothing to do with laughing at either Kristin or anyone else.

Kristin still believed that her coworker was performing poorly, but now she wasn't so quick to take that behavior personally. Kristin became more able say to herself, "This is just the way she is, at least for now; and even though I'd like her to change, she may not. I don't need to be her friend, and I have other coworkers whom I can depend on, so I'll just do my job." Saying this to herself freed Kristin to focus on her own job and on getting her own needs met at work. At first, during particular crunch times when everyone needed to work harder and act more cooperatively, Kristin found herself having to remember that imaginary conversation. After a while, though, as she focused more on other coworkers (especially the ones she could count on, the ones who shared her work ethic and appreciated and matched her efforts), her formerly upsetting coworker simply became part of her work situation rather than a focus of her time and energy.

As Kristin found, part of the benefit of this step is that, by seeing plausible reasons for the other person's actions and gaining distance from the experience as a result, we become free to see possibilities that our anger may have obscured from our view. Thus, releasing her focus on the problematic coworker allowed Kristin to see her other coworkers more clearly. Doing so, rather than simply finding coworkers who shared her anger, she found those who made her job both easier and more enjoyable.

Anger locks you into a relationship with the person with whom you are upset, repeatedly guiding your attention back to your memory of who and what has distressed you. The gift-of-anger process incrementally unlocks your imprisoned focus and provides you with the internal strength to move beyond the experience, freeing you to reevaluate your association with the other person as well. So, as you complete this step, you will most likely notice that your own distressing experience is no longer grasping so fervently at your attention. It is no longer center stage. Instead, it is becoming a part of your past and you are becoming someone who is growing beyond it.

Recall that Kristin didn't feel the need to befriend her problematic coworker. As you reach this step in your own process, you can also realize that using this process doesn't mean that you have to end up having a relationship with the other person. The purpose of this process is to help you to widen your frame of reference by developing your capacity to see yourself and the world around you more accurately and fully. Doing so, feeling free from the grip of your own formerly distressing experience, you can then decide which relationships are life-enhancing for you and which may not meet your needs.

EXERCISE:
Exploring the Other Person's Frame of Reference

When you're used to taking this step, you will probably find yourself able to do it quickly and in any location. In the beginning, however, give yourself the space and solitude to concentrate on bringing into your mind the image of the offending person. Then complete the following:

1. Start by considering what you know about this person. Even if you think you know nothing, focus on him or her anyway.

2. Thinking back to the upsetting incident, recall as much as you can of the person's body language, manner, facial expressions, and words. What can you surmise from this information? For instance, did the other person seem tired or frustrated? Did it seem like something difficult had just happened to him or her? Might the other person have been feeling defensive? Might he or she have been feeling impatient, ignored, overwhelmed, or angry

at something or someone else? Often, without even knowing it, we pick up nonverbal cues to someone's personality or current behavior. Nonjudgmentally noticing the information that may come to you will help you to begin to understand the other person.

3. Continue the process by asking yourself what might have been going on in the other person's life an hour before the incident. What about a day, a week, a month, a year before the incident? A whole lifetime before the incident?

Answer the questions above with as much detail as you can. Your answers will most likely contain some conjecture, or they might even come totally from your imagination. If so, you won't know for certain how well your conclusions actually fit this particular person. Whether or not they're accurate, the answers you come up with will help you see the other person as a full human being rather than only focusing on him or her as *the problem*. More than this, you will more clearly realize what absolutely *is* true—that the other person has their own hopes and dreams and their own life struggles, limitations, unmet needs, and inaccurate beliefs. This wider view will aid you to further disengage emotionally from the angering experience and to hold it more calmly.

In the unlikely event that you cannot or will not complete this step but still feel that you have finished steps one through five, you can help yourself by completing the following exercise. Please do so without blaming yourself. This next exercise is an opportunity to learn more about yourself.

EXERCISE: If This Step Seems Impossible

If you find that you truly cannot complete the preceding exercise, write yourself a letter titled "Why I Cannot or Will Not Complete This Step." Don't just stop at saying that it hurts too much or is too offensive. Be as detailed as you can by answering what makes it too painful or offensive and what keeps those feelings in place. Go as deeply and write as completely as you can.

What you will most likely find is another unmet need that must be attended to first, before beginning this step. If so, what an important discovery you will have made! This new information will be both helpful and potentially more fully healing as you take the steps to meet this newly uncovered unmet need and then move ahead with the rest of the process.

Remember not to rush any part of this process. It isn't a race—it's a healing. Treat yourself kindly, caringly, and patiently. Then, when you have finished this step, congratulate yourself for coming so far in service of your own increased well-being.

EXERCISE:
Exploring Your Current Frame of Reference

When you have completed step six to your own satisfaction, take some time to write one more self-discovery letter, just as you wrote for step two. Without reviewing your earlier letter, use your anger journal to write down your current thoughts and feelings about what happened, what you have learned from the experience, the progress you've made from completing these steps, and how you see yourself and the other person now. Then, when you're sure you have finished, compare your new and old letters.

Completing this exercise will affirm how much wider your own frame of reference has become, how much working with your anger has benefited you. You will be able to view your increased awareness, the emotional strength you have gained, and your heightened sense of well-being. Once again, congratulate yourself for all the work you've done so far. Then, turn to the next chapter for your final step.

The Gift-of-Anger Process

Now let's do our review. Look back at the steps as a refresher or even as a way to acknowledge how far you've come. The steps are:

1. **Recognize Your Anger...**

    Learn your:

    ⑾ Physical symptoms

    ⑾ Mental patterns

    ⑾ Associated feelings

    so that you can identify your most reliable personal anger cue.

    And Regain Your Emotional Balance

    Take private time to:

    ⑾ Breathe diaphragmatically

    ⑾ Take an exercise break

    ⑾ Talk it out

    ⑾ Write a poison-pen letter

    ⑾ Or use any other method that safely releases your adrenaline without causing harm, either to yourself or to anyone else.

2. **Notice Your Thoughts and Feelings**

    ⑾ Describe the anger-provoking experience and your thoughts and feelings about it.

    ⑾ Write them out in a self-discovery letter.

3. **Give Yourself Validation**

Acknowledge that from your current frame of reference, you are *right*!

4. **Identify Your Unmet Need**

There are *always* unmet needs. These needs are *always valid*.

5. **Take Action to Meet Your Need**

- Decide how you will fill your need, and take small, manageable steps to do so.

- Congratulate yourself after each step.

6. **Explore the Other Person's Frame of Reference**

- Notice or imagine the thoughts, feelings, and unmet needs the other person may have had during the angering incident.

- Acknowledge that, given the limitations of the other person's frame of reference, he or she did the best they could at that point in time.

CHAPTER 10

Step Seven: Free Yourself with Forgiveness

Now that you've written your second self-discovery letter, exploring your current thoughts and feelings about what happened and acknowledging the awareness, emotional strength, and well-being you have gained by working deeply with your anger, you're ready to take the seventh and final step of this process. It is time to forgive the other person. "Forgiveness" is an ancient term that has been defined religiously, spiritually, and psychologically. This chapter will define forgiveness anew, exploring both its limits and its gifts.

The Limits and Gifts of Forgiveness

Some people believe that forgiveness is something you do for the other person, offering a kind of absolution that frees them from responsibility for their act and welcomes them back into your life. That, however, is far from the truth. Forgiveness is not about condoning someone else's actions, nor is it about reestablishing any relationship that you feel might in some way be harmful to you. Rather than being something you do for the other person, forgiveness is, more than anything else, a gift you give yourself. Forgiving can be a final act of setting yourself free from your previously upsetting experience so that you can wholeheartedly embrace the potential that lies before you. Let's further explore the meaning of this sometimes-elusive concept to gain a greater understanding of the goal.

A Definition of Forgiveness

To *forgive*, as used in the gift-of-anger process, has three facets. First, it means that *you accept the reality of what happened.* No longer struggling with your memory of it, you can say without an emotional charge that the event did, in fact, occur.

Second, forgiving means that you *recognize the healing and growth that you have accomplished from working with and through the experience.* You've become more than you were, and it's time to update your beliefs about yourself by affirming the wisdom and capacity you have gained from uncovering an unmet need and taking actions to meet it.

Third, forgiving means that you *wish healing and growth for the other person,* so that their frame of reference can widen and they can gain in wisdom and capacity as well. Many people are comfortable recounting what happened and claiming their resulting healing and growth, but they balk at wishing healing and growth for the other person. So, let's talk about why this part of forgiveness is valuable and important.

One reason to wish healing and growth for the other person is that doing so allows you to complete the process of taking back your own power and unhooking yourself from the hurtful incident. Having updated your belief about yourself and affirmed what you've gained from taking actions to meet your own need, you can see yourself and your own strength more accurately. While you may have felt powerless during and immediately after the incident, you can trust now that you can thrive in spite of what happened. In fact, you may well feel stronger and more peaceful because of the strength and capacity you have discovered within yourself. As you'll recall, continuing to hold negative thoughts and feelings about the other person ensures that you remain tied to them and to the angering incident. Wishing the person healing and growth instead honors your own hard and successful work. It emphasizes the fact that you have moved beyond the need to see the other person completely negatively rather than understanding that they have their own limited frame of reference. By wishing them healing and growth, you acknowledge that you have moved beyond your anger and can place the incident firmly into your past. This separation frees you to be more fully present to what is here, now.

Wishing the other person healing and growth is also an act of compassion. Recognizing that this person's frame of reference is constricted by their mistaken beliefs, you can wish them healing and growth as you wish it for everyone. In one way or another, we are all stuck in our restrictive frames until we take enough steps to free ourselves from each constriction that our mistaken, learned beliefs cause. Thus, we are all in need of compassion, healing, and growth. Having taken steps to meet one of your own needs, you can see that truth more clearly than many people, and you might wish the other person healing and growth because of what you see and know about us all.

The more we all widen our frames of reference and see each other more clearly, the less hurt we will give and receive. So, this third facet of forgiveness becomes not only a personal act of empowerment and compassion but also an act of planetary awareness. With instant access to one another through the Internet and with the ability to fly to far-off places quickly, we have an enormous impact on one another. Thus, you might wish healing and growth for the other person because you realize that our ability to impact each other joins us and gives each of us an interest in each other's well-being. You may find that you naturally wish healing and growth for the other person, that you wish it for everyone on the planet, so that we can come together more peacefully and with greater understanding.

There is one final reason to take all three actions of forgiveness. Taken together, accepting what happened without emotional charge, acknowledging your resulting healing and growth, and wishing it for the other person is a testament to the individual you have become through your commitment and your hard work. You're so much more than that one experience or that one interaction. You have not only survived it, you have grown as a result of it. You have gained increased awareness and greater emotional strength, and now, as your forgiveness sets you free to move beyond the event, you gain a deepened sense of peace as well.

When to Forgive

Depending on the seriousness of the angering experience, it may take several cycles through the first six steps before you feel ready to proceed to step seven. If you find yourself needing more time with the preceding steps, I encourage you to congratulate yourself for your willingness to stay with your process rather than hurrying yourself along or making this a right-wrong situation. The focus of this process is to increase your awareness, inner strength, and peace. One of the most important ways to gain these benefits is to acknowledge and honor your own uniqueness, including your own pace. So how do you know when you are actually ready to forgive the other person? The following exercise will tell you.

EXERCISE: Are You Ready to Forgive?

To see if you're ready to forgive the other person, describe the angering event to yourself. If you feel more anger rising up, you will benefit by repeating the first six steps. Your current anger may guide you back to the unmet need you uncovered earlier, or perhaps you'll discover another need that requires attention. Either way, continue to take small, manageable actions to meet the need or needs that you identify until you can describe your experience without feeling anger arise. Then you're ready for the final step of forgiveness.

Approaches to Forgiveness

There are two different approaches that you can choose between to forgive the other person. First, you can talk with them directly. We often become the angriest with those we love. Forgiving the other person by sitting down and talking with them face-to-face may be the perfect way to forgive if you're going to continue a relationship with this person, and especially if the relationship is a close one. Doing so may help heal whatever relationship breach has resulted from the angering event.

Alternatively, you can forgive the person in a letter. You can write this communication and send it to the person you've been angry with, or you can choose to write it in your anger journal as a testament to the healing work you've done. Again, the correct way is whichever one feels best to you. The decision is yours to make and an exercise at the end of this chapter will help you do so.

Completing the Process

Once you've chosen either to write a letter of forgiveness or to forgive in person, you're ready to bring closure to the incident. These three steps will help you forgive and move on, freeing yourself from the anger that tied you to the original angering incident.

Accept what happened. Once you can calmly acknowledge what happened without feeling anger (the first forgiveness action), and have decided on the approach, you can forgive the person by simply writing, or facing the person and saying, "I forgive you." You may choose to keep it simple or you may choose to thoroughly explain the issue for which you forgive them. You may even decide to include an affirmation of how much this person means to you, should that be the case. The decision is yours.

Trust yourself to make the decisions that work best for you. While many people wish for a hard-and-fast rule, fearing they will do it "wrong," the only rule is to say and do what feels true and right to you and to redo the gift-of-anger process if you discover further anger. Beyond that, there is no way to do this step incorrectly. You will have a sense of the wording that fits you. That's the wording to use.

Recognize your progress. The second forgiveness action is to affirm your own healing and growth. You are acknowledging that you have not only healed from the angering experience, you have grown as a result of it. Through your commitment and your hard work, you have widened your frame of reference and become more than you used to be. You can now hold the experience as part of your history, and you can move on with your life.

This second forgiveness action is one that you will not necessarily want to share with the other person, even if you have decided to speak or write directly to them. If you two are in a business relationship, for instance, discussing your growth may or may not be appropriate. However, doing so in a close, personal relationship may be important. Again, you're the only one who can decide. Whether or not you share this information with the other person, though, do affirm it for yourself. It is so important to claim your healing and celebrate who you are now that you've grown beyond your previously limited definition of yourself. As you have learned, claiming your increased wisdom, healing, and growth helps cement them more deeply into place.

Hope for healing for the other person. The third and final ingredient of forgiveness is to wish healing and growth for the person with whom you were angry. Again, you decide whether to share this with the other person or to simply affirm it in your mind. As with the other forgiveness actions, whom you share this with depends on your relationship. Either way, by taking this action you acknowledge that the other person has the potential of widening their own frame of reference and growing beyond their limitations. Affirming this potential for them, by extension, affirms it for everyone. This is a personal act of compassion. It is also a basis of hope for the world.

⫶⊩ Eric

Eric, you may recall, had been angry with his household movers for ruining many of his belongings and with the claims adjustor who tried to minimize the company's responsibility. He had also been angry with himself, believing that he should have foreseen this disaster and chosen a better moving company. After negotiating an acceptable settlement and working sufficiently with his self-directed anger (something you will learn how to do in the next chapter), Eric chose to forgive both the moving company personnel and himself by writing a letter that he then kept in his anger journal. Since he was keeping the letter, he wrote in detail about his own growth and about his wish for healing and growth for the moving company personnel as well.

It was after writing his letter that Eric realized that he no longer felt like a victim. Taking the steps in the process and completing them by writing his forgiveness letter resulted in his seeing himself as someone who was growing in awareness and in the capacity to handle problems and live more peacefully and joyfully.

Talking about it later, Eric said that the positive feelings he got from writing his letter stayed with him. He found himself appreciating other people more and acting with more awareness and kindness to those around him, as well as to himself. "I get that we're all doing our best," he said. "Sometimes the results are horrid, but the growth sure feels good. And it's great to like myself better now."

Like Eric, many people find that, after they use this process and practice forgiveness, they become less judging of themselves and of others. Feeling more at peace because of their own inner work, they behave more peacefully, both toward themselves and toward those around them.

⑪ Janet

Remember Janet? She had been angry with her doctor for not listening to or trying to understand her. Janet was ready for this final step. Having worked through her anger with her doctor and taken care of herself by talking with him about his lack of understanding during her last visit, Janet was able to appreciate her new, more assertive behavior and to see her past anger as a gift that led her to this new strength. She saw forgiveness as a natural finish to the growth process her anger had initiated.

Janet felt it was important to forgive her doctor in person if he sincerely apologized, and she came to her meeting with him prepared to do so. After he said how sorry he was, she told him that she appreciated his sincerity and understanding and that she forgave him and wanted to continue working with him. She also told him briefly of the strengths she had gained as a result of working with her anger.

Talking about it afterward, Janet said that she felt that her doctor's apology showed that he, too, had grown beyond his past behavior. Now she felt complete and able to put this negative experience with him behind her.

⅗ Kristin

Kristin, as we saw, used the gift-of-anger process because she was angry with her "lazy and selfish" coworker. For step seven, she chose to write a letter. After writing it, she kept it with her anger journal to remind herself of all that she had accomplished using this process.

Forgiving her coworker seemed to set Kristin free, at least for a while. Eventually, though, a special project caused her to become angry once again, and she returned to therapy. What came from our discussion was her realization that she had been thrown off balance by some changes in the structure of her current assignment. The increased workload had been assigned to the group in general, rather than specific tasks being assigned to specific people. As a result, Kristin had once again taken up the slack caused by her coworker's lack of effort. She also experienced a reemergence of anger and resentment.

For Kristin, the renewal of her anger became an opportunity for deeper healing and greater personal growth. She began the gift-of-anger process again and, as a result, concentrated on further developing her ability to be clearer and firmer about her limits at work. Once again, she realized that she could not affect her coworker's behavior, but she certainly could (and did) take increasingly better care of herself.

Anger arises whenever we have a need for it, inviting us to look at the opportunities for healing and growth that lie waiting beneath it. As it did for Kristin, anger often works one layer at a time, helping us heal what is there and eventually revealing what lies even deeper.

As she continued to use the process, Kristin found that she became less angry, caught it sooner, and processed her anger more quickly. She also realized that as long as her work situation held lessons for her, anger might well arise to help her pay attention, uncover her needs, and meet them.

EXERCISE: Deciding Your Approach

Consider whether you want to talk with the other person or write a letter, and if you're going to write a letter, decide whether you will send or keep it. This is a time to honor yourself, to recognize your hard work, and to celebrate your success, so choose the method that draws you most strongly. Then, having made your choice, you can forgive the other person by completing the actions in the next exercise.

EXERCISE: Forgiving the Other Person

When you are ready for this step, set aside enough quiet time to complete it fully. You might plan to leave time not only to finish your forgiveness exercise but also to journal about it, should you wish to do so.

If you can, pick a loving environment, one that feels both comfortable and peaceful to you. If you wish, add flowers or other objects that increase the sense of peace and nurturing that your environment provides. Then, choose a time when you can be free from any distractions and turn off your phone so you won't be disturbed. This is the culmination of your healing experience and a time for celebration as well. Affirm that truth in any way that seems right and proceed with the method you have chosen. These steps will help:

1. Whether you're meeting face-to-face or writing a letter, take some time to consider what you want to say. Being spontaneous can be fine, but writing out your thoughts is often a good idea so that you remember to say everything that's important to you.

2. Be sure to include each of the three forgiveness actions—stating what happened and acknowledging that you forgive the other person, acknowledging your healing and growth, and wishing healing and growth for the other person—whether you share all three actions with the other person or affirm some or all of the actions just to yourself. Use whichever words or images you have chosen.

3. Congratulate yourself for using a painful experience as an opportunity to further your own awareness and understanding. Appreciate that you have used this painful situation as a catalyst to increase your emotional strength and your sense of inner and interpersonal peace.

While forgiveness is a personal experience, it's also a global one. No matter which format you choose, your personal act of forgiveness will most likely change you in great or very subtle ways. You, in turn, will affect everyone around you—as we all do. And the people you have affected will affect everyone around them. It's highly unlikely that you will ever know all the positive changes that your act of forgiveness brings. But if you could somehow know the extent of your impact, you might be amazed at how far-reaching your act of forgiveness can be.

The Gift-of-Anger Process

We've now moved through step seven, so we can take a good look at all the steps in the gift-of-anger process together. This review can help you refresh your inspiration and can also serve as a reminder of how far you've come. Congratulations! The steps are:

1. **Recognize Your Anger...**

   Learn your:

   ⑃ Physical symptoms

⫴ Mental patterns

⫴ Associated feelings

so that you can identify your most reliable personal anger cue.

And Regain Your Emotional Balance

Take private time to:

⫴ Breathe diaphragmatically

⫴ Take an exercise break

⫴ Talk it out

⫴ Write a poison-pen letter

⫴ Or use any other method that safely releases your adrenaline without causing harm, either to yourself or to anyone else.

2. **Notice Your Thoughts and Feelings**

⫴ Describe the anger-provoking experience and your thoughts and feelings about it.

⫴ Write them out in a self-discovery letter.

3. **Give Yourself Validation**

Acknowledge that from your current frame of reference, you are *right*!

4. **Identify Your Unmet Need**

There are *always* unmet needs. These needs are *always valid*.

5. **Take Action to Meet Your Need**

⫴ Decide how you will fill your need, and take small, manageable steps to do so.

⫸ Congratulate yourself after each step.

6. Explore the Other Person's Frame of Reference

⫸ Notice or imagine the thoughts, feelings, and unmet needs the other person may have had during the angering incident.

⫸ Acknowledge that, given the limitations of the other person's frame of reference, he or she did the best they could at that point in time.

7. Free Yourself with Forgiveness

When you can recount what happened without feeling further anger:

⫸ Write or tell the other person that you forgive him or her.

⫸ Affirm your resulting healing and growth.

⫸ Wish healing and growth for the other person.

Now you're ready for the final chapter.

CHAPTER 11

When You're Angry with Yourself

You may speak more openly about being angry with others, but if you're like many people, the person you are most often angry with is yourself. You're the one from whom you expect the most. So many of us are very demanding of ourselves, knowing intellectually that perfection is impossible but feeling that we should somehow attain it anyway. We want to do things "right." Anything less can, and often does, result in self-blame. So, while your self-directed anger may be warranted, it may also be unfair or at least overdone. What would help is a way to work respectfully with this anger so that either way, justified or not, it becomes another healing tool, another guide to personal growth. That is the purpose of this chapter.

You learned earlier that anger emerges as a result of inaccurate and constricting beliefs about yourself that keep some of your needs from being met. While you may not be able to identify those beliefs directly, your painful feelings and thoughts will lead you to at least one unmet need. Then, meeting that need, you can update an inaccurate belief about yourself so that your frame of reference widens and you see yourself more accurately and more expansively. As a result, you become more aware, emotionally stronger, and more at peace. You may even find that you have less need for anger. This is the model that you've learned thus far, and it works just as well when you're angry with yourself. What changes a bit is the process. Let's take a look to see how.

The Self-Directed Gift-of-Anger Process

While there are seven steps to the gift-of-anger process when you are angry with another person, there are nine steps when you're angry with yourself. The extra steps allow you to explore two different sets of feelings leading to different needs. First, you explore your *current angry feelings* about your behavior so you can identify *what you need to do now to make amends*. Then you explore your *original feelings*, the *ones you had as you were saying and doing whatever you now regret.* Exploring your original feelings gives you the information to identify your *original unmet need,* the need that caused you to behave in a way you now dislike. As you will see, to truly heal and move on from the experience, you must uncover and meet both your current need and your original one.

Recall that when you use the gift-of-anger process because you're angry with another person, you eventually explore the other person's frame of reference so that you have at least some idea of why they behaved the way they did. Doing so gives you a fuller perspective about what actually happened. When you are angry with yourself, you also come to a step where you explore the frame of reference of the person with whom you're angry. However, this time you can really explore that person's motivations because the person you are angry with is *you*. Rather than just taking one step that may consist mostly of speculation about someone else's feelings and needs, you can delve deeply into the feelings and needs that caused the angering behavior because it was *your* behavior, caused by *your* feelings and needs.

Using the process with yourself, you begin by calming yourself enough to explore the experience as usual. You write a self-discovery letter containing your current angry thoughts and feelings about yourself and then validate what you wrote. Using this letter, you identify your current need—the one which, when met, will constitute amends for your words and actions. Then you write a second self-discovery letter, writing out your thoughts and feelings at the time you said or did what now angers you and realizing that those thoughts and feelings were your best effort at the time. Using this second letter, you can uncover your original unmet need, the one that caused you to behave as you did. Having uncovered both your current and your original needs, you can take steps to meet them both. And when you're ready, you can forgive yourself.

This longer process might sound a bit confusing, so take a look at an explanation of each step, in the order that you take it.

Step one: Recognize and discharge. Begin, as usual, by recognizing your anger and discharging your adrenaline in a safe way. This is always the first step to take when you're angry. It's the step that will move you from stage one (focusing outward, on the object of your anger) to stage two. In this second stage, you can look inward in contemplation and see beneath your surface emotions to the underlying feelings and unmet needs toward which your anger is directing you.

Step two: Write it down.. Write a self-discovery letter that focuses on your current thoughts and feelings, those that underlie your present anger with yourself. The goal here is to understand and acknowledge exactly what you believe you did wrong, thoroughly explaining what you dislike about your behavior. Identify the painful feelings that are underneath your anger—perhaps disappointment with yourself, shame, guilt, embarrassment, or any other emotions you might be feeling. Write your thoughts and feelings down fully, as you have learned to do when angry with others, being as specific and thorough as you can.

Step three: Validate. Validate for yourself that, from your frame of reference and at this point in time, you are correct. Your estimation of your behavior is accurate and you are right to be angry with yourself. As you take this step, remember that you are acknowledging the truth of how you feel about yourself based on what happened at a particular point in time. This isn't the full truth of who you are, nor is it an immutable truth. It is, instead, your acknowledgment of your own upsetting behavior and the beginning of your current opportunity for understanding and growth.

Step four: Look for the need. Identify your *current need* by asking yourself *how you wish you had behaved*. You can find your answer by focusing on the underlying feelings you wrote about in your self-discovery letter. As with your anger toward others, ask yourself, "What is the cure for these feelings?" Or you can ask yourself what you would do differently if you could start over and redo the experience. Take your time with this step. Give yourself the opportunity to describe your need accurately, just as when you are angry with another. Doing so will help you determine the small, manageable actions you can take to meet this need.

Step five: Write again. Here is where the process begins to look different. In step five, you write a second self-discovery letter. This time the focus of your letter is on the thoughts and feelings you had that seemed to justify the regrettable behavior. Take the time to uncover and really consider what the reasons for your actions were, writing out fully what your thoughts and feelings were then. You are not writing this second letter as an excuse. This letter is a way to understand your actions so that you can, a couple of steps from now, identify the unmet need that caused you to act the way you did. Then you'll be able to take steps to meet that need, too.

Perhaps, like lots of other people, you're used to just berating yourself for your behavior and telling yourself firmly not to act that way again. Doing so, however, dishonors you by implying that you were simply bad when, in fact, that isn't the case. Your actions did not occur by accident or because of "badness." Whether or not you are conscious of the unmet need driving your current, upsetting behavior, you do have one. Aware of it or not, you always act to satisfy a need. We all do. What this process does is to help you make your need known so that you can work toward meeting it in a way that both supports you and takes into account the people around you.

Step six: Validate again. Give yourself validation once again, this time validating that, from your frame of reference at the time of your original actions, your words and your behavior were correct. You did the very best you could at that time. Really affirm this to yourself. Congratulate yourself as well for taking yourself seriously and treating yourself caringly by taking the time and effort to understand your behavior more fully.

Step seven: Pinpoint the original need. Now it's time to explore what you wrote and identify your *original need, the one that caused you to behave in a way that now angers you.* You can do so in the same way you have already learned, by asking yourself what the cure would be for the painful feelings you just wrote about in your second letter. Again, give yourself time to label your unmet need in a way that feels accurate to you.

Step eight: Work to meet your needs. With your knowledge of why you behaved the way you did, along with your awareness of how you wish you had behaved, you have the information to meet both of your needs—the original unmet need that caused your behavior and your current need to make amends. With this information, you can begin to identify and take the small, manageable actions that will lead you to meet your needs and enable you to forgive yourself.

Remember that as you take each small action toward fulfilling your needs, it is important to congratulate yourself. Doing so not only acknowledges your actions, it also celebrates the fact that your frame of reference is widening so that you see yourself and others more accurately and fully. You are growing, literally becoming more than you used to be. Becoming more conscious of your true needs and how to meet them, you become more skilled in responding to difficulty in a way that both satisfies your own needs and honors your personal beliefs about how you want to treat yourself and others.

Step nine: Forgive. Forgiveness is, as always, your final step. You'll know that you're ready for this step in two ways: when you can say, without anger, that the event occurred and when you can recognize the healing and growth that you have accomplished from working with and through this experience. When you're ready, you can forgive yourself, as you do others, either in person or in a letter. The exercise at the end of this chapter will explain how.

Now that you have the rationale for the steps to take when you're angry with yourself and an explanation of each step in order, take a look at how others have used these steps to understand and work through their own self-directed anger.

⑪ Karen

Karen was angry with herself for the way she had raised her son Peter. Though Peter was twenty-six years old, Karen blamed herself for the fact that he had difficulty acting independently. Peter was currently having a tough time following through with his desire to change jobs, and Karen believed that her poor parenting was the cause of his indecisiveness. With her blame and anger at herself in mind, Karen began the self-directed gift-of-anger process.

She completed step one by releasing her adrenaline through diaphragmatic breathing. Then she took some time to examine her current angry thoughts and feelings in step two by writing her first self-discovery letter. In her letter, Karen wrote about how she had always been there for Peter, helping him reach his goals. In fact, she had reached more than a few of those goals for him, identifying the necessary steps and taking them herself. Peter had grown up knowing that he could count on his mom to do much of his work. "I took over so often," she wrote. "How did I think he was ever going to learn to help himself? I've been a pushy, know-it-all, smothering mom, unwilling to let my kid grow up."

Reading her letter, Karen completed step three by unhappily acknowledging to herself that what she had written was true. She had taken over much of her son's life, making it harder for him to learn to do things for himself. "I'm clearly right to be angry with myself," she admitted.

Next, turning to step four, Karen identified the unmet need in her current relationship with her son. She saw her need to step back and allow Peter the practice necessary to become an independent adult.

At this point, Karen was ready for step five. She wrote her second self-discovery letter to explore the thoughts and feelings that had led her to take over for Peter when he was growing up. From this perspective, Karen told a different story.

She began by considering her own childhood, noting that her parents had moved frequently. As a result, they were usually focused on getting themselves established in each new community, spending little time with their daughter. Karen wrote about her loneliness growing up and her wish that her parents would have paid more attention to her and helped her more. She noted that she had promised herself to treat her own children differently.

"I didn't want my son to have to go through what I went through," she wrote. "I wanted Peter to know that I was there for him." She acknowledged as well that the man she had married had been kind but distant, much like her own parents had been. She hadn't received his help in parenting Peter, which contributed to her impulse to focus so intently on her son.

Reviewing her second letter in step six, Karen began to see her parenting in a more balanced way. She acknowledged to herself that she had made her decisions about helping Peter with the best of intentions. She also recognized that Peter was, in many ways, doing quite well. Karen might not have had all the skills she would have wished for as a parent, but she'd certainly had many.

In step seven, Karen identified and labeled her original need to make sure her son knew that she was there for him and would help as much as she could. "I wanted so much to give him what I hadn't had that I went overboard and gave him too much help. He knows I care. Now I need to let him know that I care about him enough to let him reach his own goals."

Karen completed step eight by beginning to come up with a plan. She made a commitment to herself to start more effectively parenting Peter by letting him set his own pace and congratulating him for each step he took toward reaching his goal himself. This, she decided, was how she could best make amends. She knew that allowing Peter his independence would require lessening her own dependence on him and his success. Karen needed to make commitments that would use her time

163

in a worthwhile manner rather than focusing so singularly on Peter. "I want to find a way to continue to use my skills to help others," she wrote, "but now I want it to be mutual. This time I want to do something where others help me, too."

After several small, manageable, preparatory steps, Karen chose a volunteer opportunity in which she could work as part of a team. She then sat down with Peter and explained what she had learned and what changes she was making as a result. She apologized for having taken over so often, explaining that it stemmed from her own background and not from any mistrust of him. She then talked about setting goals in her own life, emphasizing the importance of breaking goals into small, doable actions and congratulating herself each step of the way.

Expressing trust in her son, Karen offered to help Peter if he asked. "I'll always be there for you, Peter," she said. "If I can, I'll give you whatever help that you ask me for. But I'll do my best not to get in your way or take over and do the work for you. From now on, I want to learn to celebrate with you as you take your own steps." Then Karen forgave herself in a letter to herself that she wrote into her journal.

Elaine

Elaine was sixty years old and overweight, with increasingly debilitating physical symptoms. Having consulted her doctor about how to become more physically healthy, she decided that she also wanted to work on her anger toward herself.

"I stopped exercising a couple of years ago," she lamented, "and I began treating myself to junk food instead. I just felt like I was getting old and so it didn't matter anyway. Now I'm a mess and it's all my fault. I can't believe I did this to myself."

Writing her first self-discovery letter focusing on her angry feelings was difficult for Elaine. It wasn't just that she blamed herself. What hurt more was how ashamed she felt and how hopeless. "I tried to exercise yesterday and couldn't," she said dejectedly. "I have an elliptical machine at home that used to be so easy to use, but now I can't even manage two minutes.

How could I do this to myself? I'm not sure I even deserve to get better."

Validating her self-blame and shame in step three was easy, as was step four. "I know what I need to do to make amends," Elaine said. "I need to exercise regularly and eat real food instead of junk. I can say that with no problem, but doing it—that's where it gets tough."

Coming to step five, Elaine wrote her second self-discovery letter, focusing on the thoughts and feelings that had caused her to stop exercising and overeat junk food. In this letter she wrote about how bored she was; how tired she was of following a routine she had maintained for far too long and that now seemed empty. "There just doesn't seem to be enough spark in life anymore," she said, talking about the feelings her letter brought up. "One day is pretty much like the next."

Validating her thoughts and feelings in step six was sad for Elaine, as she looked directly at her painful issues. Then, in step seven, she identified her needs to find some ways to enjoy her life again, as well as to exercise and eat more healthfully. "I don't believe in suicide," she said, "and I may have a lot more years left. I sure don't want to keep living them like this." With that thought, she began to consider what steps she could take—tiny steps that she could manage in her current physical and emotional shape.

Elaine took one very small, manageable action at a time toward health and well-being, renewing her commitment each day and congratulating herself with each success. Then, whenever she backslid (as we all do), she reviewed her needs and began again. As a result, she made fairly steady progress toward her goals. A year later, she was healthier than she'd been and much closer to her ideal weight. She had also identified and slowly begun to do some work that she found increasingly fulfilling. She had forgiven herself as well, completing this last step by saying her forgiveness out loud as she looked directly into her own eyes in a mirror.

Blame, Guilt, Shame, and Hopelessness

Elaine's initial reaction to not being able to exercise for even two minutes was typical of many people's, and it had the same results. Suddenly concerned about a long-term problem, she wanted the problem fixed *now*. When that proved impossible, she was left facing the feelings she had hoped to avoid: blame, guilt, shame, and hopelessness.

These emotions form a downward spiral too easily traveled. Blaming ourselves, many of us say, "It's *all* my fault. I caused this." What often emerges next is guilt. When guilt arises, we may say, "I've really messed up, and I don't know if I can make it right." Then, if shame takes over, we translate our concern into a deeper and more invasive and pervasive belief, "I've messed up, and I can't make *me* right." Elaine illustrated a variation of this when she said, "I'm not sure I even deserve to get better." What so often follows is hopelessness.

Blame, guilt, and shame are important and valuable feelings, both as indicators of hurtful actions taken and as calls to change. However, they are frequently misused by being applied to the whole person rather than to a specific behavior, and to all of time, rather than just to the present. When that happens, these emotions tend to feel like a life sentence instead of an acknowledgment of a specific behavior that has caused specific hurt or harm, an acknowledgment of the state one is in right now.

Focused on a behavior rather than a whole person, these painful feelings can initiate a reevaluation and correction of one's actions. Used to describe the whole person forever, though, they become all encompassing and can hold that person immobile. What results is a sense of hopelessness.

Elaine, for example, after appropriately blaming herself for her physical condition, fell into believing that *she* was a problem—and possibly unworthy of a solution. Blaming herself, ashamed of herself, and now hopeless, she simply felt stuck. Not only did she not know the way to move beyond her feelings, she wasn't sure there *was* a way. What she learned is that it is neither accurate nor helpful to apply blame to ourselves as a whole person, but only to those actions that need correction. She also learned that we are not meant to stay stuck in an emotion.

In some cases, the vastness of the wrong you may have committed may seem to require that you blame yourself as a whole and may seem to ensure that you will stay stuck in your blame, shame, and hopelessness. Yet, even then, staying stuck is not the answer. Consider Mark.

⫴ Mark

A colleague told a story of what happened when she attended a gathering to listen to a spiritual teacher. She explained that another attendee, whom we will call Mark, disclosed the fact that he once took actions that resulted in the death of a friend. In the years following, he loaded himself down with feelings of self-blame, and guilt, and shame. How could there be a way beyond these feelings? He felt hopeless.

The spiritual teacher told him to devote himself to helping as many people as possible. By consciously focusing on helping others, he would, in the best way he could, be honoring his friend. He would be respecting his own life as well, rather than devaluing it by remaining stuck in self-blame, guilt, shame, and hopelessness.

What has already happened is done, and if it cannot be undone, then it must be accepted as fact—even if that fact is tragic. It doesn't mean that you condone what happened. It means you accept that it *did* happen. Now, starting where you are, take one small, manageable step at a time to make amends in the best and most caring way you can devise.

The Value of At-Onement

In an example as serious as Mark's, it seems appropriate to talk not about making amends, but about atoning. If you take the word "atone" apart, it becomes two words, "at one." *Atonement* means "at-onement," *the state of feeling at one with yourself and with others in your life.*

In preparing to take actions to meet the needs of any relationship, whether it's with yourself or with another, you are really asking yourself, "What needs to happen in order to feel at one?" For Elaine, in the earlier example, the answer was, "I need to feel healthy and to know that I can take care of myself in a healthy way. I also need to be involved in fulfilling relationships. Then I'll feel at one with myself and with others." For Mark, in the last example, the answer was to do what he could to honor his friend's life and to honor the fact that the rest of his own life was yet to be lived.

As many have learned, this is actually a question worth asking periodically: "Am I feeling at one with myself and with the world around me now? If not, what needs to happen for me to feel more positively and peacefully connected?" Ask yourself this question and act on your answer using the small, manageable steps this process teaches, congratulating yourself each step of the way. As you do so, your actions will bring you closer and closer to feeling at one with yourself and with the world around you.

EXERCISE: Practicing the Self-Directed Gift-of-Anger-Process

You can use this process any time you're angry with yourself. As you see from the examples above, doing so can widen your frame of reference, allowing you to more accurately and fully see and fulfill both your own original need and the needs of the current situation. Take these steps:

1. Begin by finding a quiet place where you will be undisturbed. Discharge any adrenaline you may feel, using whatever method is comfortable for you.

2. Notice your angry thoughts and feelings, preferably taking time to write them down in your journal as part of a self-discovery letter. Your goal is to describe the anger-provoking experience so that you can identify what you believe you did wrong.

3. Validate that, from your current frame of reference, you are right to be angry with yourself.

4. Identify the cure—the current need that, when filled, would make amends.

5. Write your second self-discovery letter, exploring the thoughts and feelings that compelled you to act in a way you now disapprove of.

6. Acknowledge that your actions were correct to the best of your ability, given your frame of reference at the time.

7. Review your second letter and identify your original unmet need, taking the time to label it in a way that feels right to you.

8. Decide what three small, manageable actions you will take to begin to meet both of your needs and, taking these actions, congratulate yourself each small step of the way. Then, choose three more small, manageable actions and continue the process until you feel complete.

9. When you've taken sufficient actions to feel ready to forgive yourself, you can do so by writing a letter to yourself in your anger journal. Be sure to include telling yourself that you forgive yourself and exploring how you have used this experience as a healing tool, growing in your awareness and capacity as a result of it.

You also have the option to speak your forgiving words as you look directly at yourself in a mirror, so you can truly see whom you are forgiving. Speak to yourself as you would to anyone whom you care enough about to forgive in person. This can be a very powerful method. Many people have said that they don't like looking at themselves for long. Others say that they don't like looking at themselves at all. If you feel this way, you might especially want to use a mirror as a way of beginning to move into acceptance of yourself as the well-meaning and valuable person that you are.

Mistakes are a given if you are human, and sometimes a mistake can be catastrophic. No matter how big or small, however, each mistake has the potential to initiate a path back to at-onement. Each mistake can become a healing tool, helping you to grow in awareness, strengthen emotionally, and deepen your sense of inner and interpersonal peace. As you take the steps to make that happen, you may find that you are growing in acceptance and appreciation of yourself, as well as more fully accepting and appreciating those around you.

Some Final Thoughts and Wishes

Now that you've read the book and done the exercises, you see firsthand that your anger can be a beneficial guide to your own well-being. You now understand the two stages of anger, and you've practiced using it to uncover and begin to meet your own unmet needs. You can clearly see the value of your anger as a pathway to increasing your awareness and your true emotional strength—the way anger can actually enhance your sense of inner and interpersonal peace. This is the potential of anger in stage two. This is anger's gift to you.

I'm hoping that you've also learned that none of your emotions is *bad*. Though some certainly feel better than others, all of them exist to help you. *All of your emotions are in your service.* Using them as guides to your unmet needs, you can identify and begin to meet those needs, automatically correcting your mistaken beliefs that have held those needs in place. Your frame of reference widens as you take these steps, and your ability to hold and work with your tough experiences more calmly and thoughtfully increases as a result.

It's important to remember that using the gift-of-anger process is hard work and takes time. You will probably find that you fall back into blaming at one point or another, perhaps frequently. When you do, stick with this process. Imagine that you're in a gym—not one that builds the capacity of your physical muscles, but one that builds your mental and emotional capacity. Each moment that you can clearly hold the reality that whomever you're angry with also has a way of seeing the world based on a frame of reference that seems valid to him or her, you're building valuable mental and emotional muscles. Each time you acknowledge that every person has their own unmet needs resulting from their own potentially mistaken beliefs, you grow stronger. You become more able to walk through life with less anger and with more compassion, both for yourself and for the people around you.

Healing old wounds with the increased understanding that the gift-of-anger process generates helps widen your frame of reference, making it more objectively accurate. Consciously substituting new behavior that is more appropriate to your widening frame of reference further lessens your need for anger. As you reenact this new, healthy pattern, congratulating yourself each time you do so, the new pattern will slowly transform from a conscious effort to an automatic habit. With what results? As Stacy, a former client, explained, "Now, when addressing issues and emotions, I become more curious than judgmental. I see how much I've softened to circumstances that used to leave me so irritated. I know that this is a direct result of the work I've done."

Like others before her, Stacy didn't just create her new behavior in a single step. She did it over time, coming closer to the behavior she hoped for each time she used the process. Gradually she found herself increasingly able to respond with curiosity and compassion rather than so frequently needing to react in judgment and anger. Congratulating herself each step of the way, she watched her frame of reference widen as she continued working with her anger.

Like Stacy, you will keep growing as you continue to use the process. This is not a race, nor is it a competition. This gift-of-anger process is about allowing your emotions space so that you can notice them, explore them, and heal from the ones that require it. This work is also about realizing that you are more than your feelings and more than your needs. Working with them, you can become more adept at holding them rather than being held hostage by them.

Equally important is the awareness that you cannot see everything. You are still always viewing life through a frame of reference, and every frame has its limits. If you know that, then you can avoid the common mistake of believing that whatever you see at any given time is the absolute truth.

Anger emerges automatically when the circumstances in your life, coupled with your beliefs about those circumstances, warrant it. Your anger will remain available when and where you need it. It will continue to offer you its power boost of protection in stage one and signal you that further healing is available in stage two. Then, if you use your anger as a guide, it will continue to lead you to the treasure of your own increased wisdom, healing, and growth.

What will most likely change is your relationship to your anger. Seeing that (as with all of your emotions) anger is always in your service, you will hopefully come to value it and to use it in a way that serves you well. As you do so, your experience of anger will most likely diminish in both frequency and intensity. You will have less need of it as you heal and will quickly take advantage of its guidance when it does emerge.

If you follow this process with commitment, will you eliminate your anger completely? I don't think so. Life is not something we can master. What we *can* master is the process of living so that, through ongoing self-exploration and course correction, we can move ever more peacefully toward our goals.

Peace, like anger, is an inside job. It begins in you and in me, and through our actions, it affects everyone with whom we come in contact. By using your anger as a starting point for your own inner healing and growth, you come to embody peace. By your individual example, you teach this process to others. We are always teaching each other through the model of our behavior. Each one of us, every moment, is a teacher. May you use your anger in a way that furthers your inner healing and personal growth. And may you, by your example, teach peace in the world.

References

Ellis, A. and R. A. Harper. 1997. *A Guide to Rational Living*. Chatsworth, CA: Wilshire Book Company.

Goleman, D. 1995. *Emotional Intelligence: Why It Can Matter More Than IQ*. New York, NY: Bantam Books.

Hanson, R. and R. Mendius. 2009. *Buddha's Brain: The Practical Neuroscience of Happiness, Love & Wisdom*. Oakland, CA: New Harbinger Publications, Inc.

Jantz, G.. 1999. *Becoming Strong Again: How to Regain Emotional Health*. Ada, MI: Baker Book House.

Langer, E. J. 1989. *Mindfulness*. Cambridge, MA: Da Capo Press.

Pert, C. 1997. *Molecules of Emotion*. New York, NY: Simon & Schuster.

Phillips, P. 1998. Study Says Stay Calm and Halve Risk of Stroke. *The Journal of the American Medical Association*. 279(16):1246-1248.

Contact the Author

I'd like to hear from you about your experiences using the gift-of-anger process. If you have stories you'd like to share or questions you want to ask, you can reach me by e-mail at marcia@giftofanger.com or at my website, www.giftofanger.com.

I offer talks and workshops based on the gift-of-anger process and would be happy to send you information and a current schedule. I'm also happy to talk with you about setting up a talk or workshop for your organization or group. Let me know if you're interested, using the e-mail address or website above.

Marcia Cannon, Ph.D., MFT, is a marriage and family therapist who has taught people how to use their anger positively for more than fifteen years. She lives in the San Francisco Bay Area and conducts talks and workshops on the gift of anger process for organizations and groups nationwide. For a current schedule of talks and workshops, or to have Cannon speak at your event, please e-mail marcia@giftofanger .com or visit www.giftofanger.com.

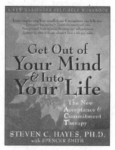

APR   2011